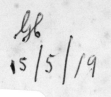

ON ENGLAND

ON ENGLAND

And other Addresses

THE RIGHT HONOURABLE

STANLEY BALDWIN, M.P.

FIRST LORD OF THE TREASURY AND PRIME MINISTER
OF GREAT BRITAIN

PHILIP ALLAN & CO. LTD.
QUALITY COURT

First impression April 1926.
Second impression May 1926.
Third impression May 1926.
Fourth impression July 1926.
Fifth impression October 1926.
Cheap Edition April 1927.

PRINTED IN GREAT BRITAIN BY ROBERT MACLEHOSE AND CO. LTD.
THE UNIVERSITY PRESS, GLASGOW.

PREFACE

I HAVE allowed, with some misgivings, some of the speeches or extracts from speeches made by me in the last two years or so to be put together in the following pages. They were in general delivered amidst the press of thronging duties and urgent preoccupations, and in this book they appear as the faithful reporter set them down at the moment of delivery. Without revision subsequently, without at the time the advantage of the *ultima manus*, they must not be judged as the leisured product of the study now that they are brought together in the fashion of a book.

It is a sound, if onerous, tradition which compels our public men to travel beyond the bounds of Party and to interpret, so far as each has power, the thought and striving of the Nation at its best, whether in politics, in industry, in art or in the practice of charity.

Public speeches are of use if they lead men to dwell on the thoughts of service to their country and of help to one another : and if these lingering echoes of former words of mine avail, in however small a measure, towards that end, those who wished to publish this book will have been justified.

STANLEY BALDWIN.

10 Downing Street,
7th April, 1926.

CONTENTS

CONTENTS

THE RIGHT HONOURABLE
STANLEY BALDWIN

29th Feb.	1908.	Mr. Baldwin succeeds his father as Member for Bewdley.
6th Dec.	1916.	Resignation of Mr. Asquith and formation of 2nd Coalition Government by Mr. Lloyd George. Mr. Bonar Law becomes Chancellor of the Exchequer.
22nd Dec.	1916.	Mr. Baldwin is appointed Parliamentary Secretary to Mr. Bonar Law.
30th Jan.	1917.	Becomes Junior Lord of the Treasury.
18th June,	1917.	Becomes Joint Financial Secretary to the Treasury.
4th Dec.	1918.	General Election.
17th March,	1921.	Mr Bonar Law resigns office in the Coalition Government.
1st April,	1921.	Mr. Baldwin appointed President of the Board of Trade.
19th Oct.	1922.	Carlton Club Meeting.
19th Oct.	1922.	Mr. Lloyd George resigns.
24th Oct.	1922.	Mr. Bonar Law forms his Government.
24th Oct.	1922.	Mr. Baldwin becomes Chancellor of the Exchequer.
20th May,	1923.	Mr. Bonar Law resigns.
22nd May,	1923.	Mr. Baldwin becomes Prime Minister.
28th May,	1923.	Mr. Baldwin elected Leader of the Unionist Party.
25th Oct.	1923.	Mr. Baldwin's speech at Plymouth on Protection.
6th Dec.	1923.	General Election.
22nd Jan.	1924.	Mr. Baldwin resigns.
29th Oct.	1924.	General Election.
4th Nov.	1924.	Mr. Baldwin again becomes Prime Minister

ON ENGLAND AND THE WEST

ENGLAND

At the Annual Dinner of the Royal Society of St. George, at the Hotel Cecil

6th May, 1924

THOUGH I do not think that in the life of a busy man there could be placed into his hands a more difficult toast than this, yet the first thought that comes into my mind as a public man is a feeling of satisfaction and profound thankfulness that I may use the word " England " without some fellow at the back of the room shouting out " Britain." I have often thought how many of the most beautiful passages in the English language would be ruined by that substitution which is so popular to-day. I read in your Dinner-book, " When God wants a hard thing done, He tells it," not to His Britons, but " to His Englishmen." And in the same way, to come to a very modern piece of poetry, how different it would be with the altered ending, " For in spite of all temptations to belong to other nations, he remains a Briton."

We have to-night to celebrate our country and our Patron Saint. It always seems to me no mere chance that besides being the Patron Saint of England, St. George was the Patron Saint of those gallant sailors around the shores of the Adriatic, and that in his honour there exists one of the most beautiful chapels in Venice to-day. The Patron Saint of sailors is surely the most suitable Patron Saint for men of the English stock ; and I think to-night amongst ourselves we might for a minute or two look at those characteristics, contradictory often, peculiar as we believe, in that great stock of which we are all members.

The Englishman is all right as long as he is content to be what God made him, an Englishman, but gets into trouble when he tries to be something else. There are chroniclers, or were chroniclers, who said it was the apeing of the French manners by our English ancestors that made us the prey of William the Norman, and led to our defeat at Hastings. Let that be a warning to us not to ape any foreign country. Let us be content to trust ourselves and to be ourselves.

Now, I always think that one of the most curious contradictions about the English stock is this : that while the criticism that is often made of us is not without an element of truth, and that is that as a nation we are less open to the intellectual sense than the Latin races, yet though that may be a fact, there is no nation on earth that has had the same knack of producing geniuses. It is almost a characteristic of the English race ; there is hardly any line in which the nation has not produced geniuses, and in a nation which many people might think restrained, unable to express itself, in this same nation you have a literature second to none that has ever existed in the world, and certainly in poetry supreme.

Then, for a more personal characteristic, we grumble, and we always have grumbled, but we never worry. Now, there is a very great truth in that, because there are foreign nations who worry but do not grumble. Grumbling is more superficial, leaves less of a mark on the character, and just as the English schoolboy, for his eternal salvation, is impervious to the receipt of learning, and by that means preserves his mental faculties further into middle age and old age than he otherwise would (and I may add that I attribute the possession of such faculties as I have to the fact that I did not overstrain them in youth), just as the Englishman has a mental reserve owing to that gift given him at his birth by St. George, so, by the absence of worry he keeps his nervous system sound and sane, with the result that in times of emergency the nervous system stands when the nervous system of other peoples breaks.

The Englishman is made for a time of crisis, and for a time of emergency. He is serene in difficulties, but may seem to be indifferent when times are easy. He may not look ahead, he may not heed warnings, he may not prepare, but when he once starts he is persistent to the death, and he is ruthless in action.

It is these gifts that have made the Englishman what he is, and that have enabled the Englishman to make England and the Empire what it is.

It is in staying power that he is supreme, and fortunately, being, as I have said, to some extent impervious to intellectual impressions as a nation, he is equally impervious to criticism—a most useful thing for an English statesman. That may be the reason why English statesmen sometimes last longer than those who are not English. I admit that in past generations we carried that virtue to an excess, and by a rebound the sins of the fathers are being visited on the children. For instance, there was a time when this particular epithet was more in vogue in political society, and the Englishman invariably spoke of the " damned " foreigner. Those days are gone, but the legacy has come to us in this, that by the swing of the pendulum we have in this country what does not exist in any other, a certain section of our people who regard every country as being in the right except their own. It largely arises, I think, among a section of the population who hold beliefs which they cannot persuade their fellow-countrymen to adopt.

There is yet one other point. I think the English people are at heart and in practice the kindest people in the world. With some faults on which I have touched, there is in England a profound sympathy for the under-dog. There is a brotherly and a neighbourly feeling which we see to a remarkable extent through all classes. There is a way of facing misfortunes with a cheerful face. It was shown to a marvellous degree in the war, and in spite of all that he said in criticism of his own people, Ruskin said one thing of immortal truth. He said : " The English laugh is the purest and truest in the metal that can be minted. And indeed only Heaven can know what the country owes to it." There is a profound truth in that. As long as a people can laugh, they are preserved from the grosser vices of life, political and moral. And as long as they can laugh, they can face all the ills that fortune may bring upon them.

Then, in no nation more than the English is there a diversified individuality. We are a people of individuals, and a people of character. You may take the writings of one of the greatest and one of the most English of writers, Charles Dickens, and you will find that practically all his characters are English. They are all different, and each of us that has gone through this world with his eyes open and his heart open, has met every one of Dickens's characters in some position or another in life. Let us see to it that we never allow our individuality as Englishmen to be steam-rollered. The preservation of the individuality of the Englishman is essential to the preservation of the type of the race, and if our differences are smoothed out and we lose that great gift, we shall lose at the same time our power. Uniformity of type is a bad thing. I regret very much myself the uniformity of speech.   Time was, two centuries ago, when you could have told by his speech from what part of England every member of Parliament came. He spoke the speech of his fathers, and I regret that the dialects have gone, and I regret that by a process which for want of a better name we have agreed among ourselves to call education, we are drifting away from the language of the people and losing some of the best English words and phrases which have lasted in the country through centuries, to make us all talk one uniform and inexpressive language.

Now, I have very little more that I want to say to you to-night, but on an occasion like this I suppose there is no one who does not ask himself in his heart and is a little shy of expressing it, what it is that England stands for to him, and to her.   And there comes into my mind a wonder as to what England may stand for in the minds of generations to come if our country goes on during the next generation as she has done in the last two, in seeing her fields converted into towns.

To me, England is the country, and the country is England.   And when I ask myself what I mean by England, when I think of England when I am abroad, England comes to me through my various senses—through the ear, through the eye, and through certain imperishable scents.   I will tell you what they are, and there may be those among you who feel as I do.

The sounds of England, the tinkle of the hammer on the anvil in the country smithy, the corncrake on a dewy morning, the sound of the scythe against the whetstone, and the sight of a plough team coming over the brow of a hill, the sight that has been seen in England since England was a land, and may be seen in England long after the Empire has perished and every works in England has ceased to function, for centuries the one eternal sight of England. The wild anemones in the woods in April, the last load at night of hay being drawn down a lane as the twilight comes on, when you can scarcely distinguish the figures of the horses as they take it home to the farm, and above all, most subtle, most penetrating and most moving, the smell of wood smoke coming up in an autumn evening, or the smell of the scutch fires : that wood smoke that our ancestors, tens of thousands of years ago, must have caught on the air when they were coming home with the result of the day's forage, when they were still nomads, and when they were still roaming the forests and the plains of the continent of Europe. These things strike down into the very depths of our nature, and touch chords that go back to the beginning of time and the human race, but they are chords that with every year of our life sound a deeper note in our innermost being.

These are the things that make England, and I grieve for it that they are not the childish inheritance of the majority of the people to-day in our country. They ought to be the inheritance of every child born

into this country, but nothing can be more touching
than to see how the working man and woman after
generations in the towns will have their tiny bit of
garden if they can, will go to gardens if they can, to
look at something they have never seen as children,
but which their ancestors knew and loved. The
love of these things is innate and inherent in our
people. It makes for that love of home, one of the
strongest features of our race, and it is that that makes
our race seek its new home in the Dominions overseas, where they have room to see things like this
that they can no more see at home. It is that power
of making homes, almost peculiar to our people, and
it is one of the sources of their greatness. They go
overseas, and they take with them what they learned
at home : love of justice, love of truth, and the
broad humanity that are so characteristic of English
people. It may well be that these traits on which
we pride ourselves, which we hope to show and try
to show in our own lives, may survive—survive
among our people so long as they are a people—and
I hope and believe this, that just as to-day more than
fifteen centuries since the last of those great Roman
legionaries left England, we still speak of the Roman
strength, and the Roman work, and the Roman character, so perhaps in the ten thousandth century, long
after the Empires of this world as we know them
have fallen and others have risen and fallen, and risen
and fallen again, the men who are then on this earth
may yet speak of those characteristics which we

prize as the characteristics of the English, and that long after, maybe, the name of the country has passed away, wherever men are honourable and upright and persevering, lovers of home, of their brethren, of justice and of humanity, the men in the world of that day may say, " We still have among us the gifts of that great English race."

MY NATIVE TOWN

AT BEWDLEY

8th August, 1925

I HAVE assisted at many functions during recent years, but at none more calculated to touch the hidden springs of the heart than that in which I have participated to-day. Bewdley, as most of you know, was in distant ages a sanctuary town to which a man, whatever his sins, might flee and be safe from justice. So whenever the rude waves of the outside world buffet me with more than usual vigour, I have only to remember that in Bewdley there is a sanctuary even for a Prime Minister.

This day has, at any rate, shown that there can be an exception to the truth contained in the words, " A prophet is not without honour, save only in his own country." I have never failed to find in my own country understanding, sympathy and support, and even when life seems most difficult and the fences in front unclimbable, I can turn back in memory and recollection to this peaceful spot by the side of the river, where I first drew breath, and in the memory of which I am able to draw strength.

There could have been no more typical English surroundings in which to cherish the earliest memories. I remember as a child looking up the river from the bridge into that mysterious and romantic land of Shropshire, so close to us, from which my people came only three generations before, and watching the smoke of the train running along the little railway through places bearing names like Wyre Forest, Cleobury Mortimer, Neen Sollars and Tenbury—names steeped in romance and redolent of the springtime of an England long ago passed, but whose heritage is ours. Those names must have been familiar to Langland as he lay on the slopes of the Malvern Hills while the great poem of *Piers Plowman* shaped itself in his brain. I remember, too, the thrill of names like The Welch Gate and The Warden of the Marches, which brought back to me even in childhood days the fact that Bewdley, long before it was incorporated in Worcestershire, was one of the most important towns in the great Marches separating Wales from England ; the title of Lord Warden of the Marches seemed to me most romantic and dignified. There were memories, too, of the long-forgotten strife between Welsh and English, of Ludlow, where the big castle still stood, and of Woodbury Hill where Owen Glendower came before the great fight beneath its slope, as the result of which the bones of English and Welsh have lain in common ground for five centuries. And one has seen how warfare may yield to peace.

It may be the recollection of those far-off days, and the intimate connection which we in the Marches had with Welshmen, that has given me a kind of affection for them, and even a sneaking affection, after all that has passed, for the greatest living Welshman, Mr. Lloyd George. I have often felt that if it were possible for His Majesty to revive the great title of Lord Warden of the Marches, I would like him to offer it to Mr. Lloyd George, on condition that he lived for three months in the year in Bewdley.

My friend the present Mayor of Bewdley has long been honourably associated with a house called The Old Pack Horse. That name reminds me of a day before grass grew on the wharves of the Severn, when Bewdley and not Liverpool was the natural export depot for Manchester, and when strings of pack-horses used to come down from Lancashire to discharge their goods at Bewdley's wharves into the " prows " which went down daily to Bristol for export to all parts of the world. Manchester and Liverpool were then smaller towns than Kidderminster is to-day. The Bridgwater Canal had not been made, and I have no doubt that in the early years of the eighteenth century the name of Bewdley was as well known in England as the names of those cities.

I think it is good for us, on an occasion like this, to dwell on these things, which show the continuity of history and bring before us the progress and the changing fortunes of our country. I spoke of the grass that has grown on the wharves on Severnside. That is true. But we still have Severn with us, and I think Severn can teach us something to-day. Rising on the slopes of Plinlimmon, she has flowed from and through Wales into England, and through our part of England. For centuries she served as a boundary and dividing line, respected by Rome and by the Celt; yet the time came when she was no longer a dividing line, but the proof of union and friendship; and while long years ago she poured her waters through country full of strife and fighting, she now waters peaceful meadows and passes through peaceful towns, with dismantled castles. It may well be that, just as she has seen strife in this country turn to peace, so again to-day, in an age when the clouds are heavy and charged with electricity, she may once more see the storm pass. But she reminds us that these things change and are effaced like the eddies on her stream; and, as of old, her deep waters will flow on through Bewdley, carrying their peace to the dwellers on Severnside, and their healing message into the heart of England.

STOURPORT

AT STOURPORT
12th January, 1925

I SUPPOSE there have been many ceremonies at which I have been present which were more magnificent than this, and made much more noise in the world, but I have never been to one that has touched me more, or one in which all the elements that can grip the heart of man can have been more present. It is a curious feeling to come down to one's own home, and to receive in one's lifetime a tribute like this of affection and goodwill, not only from one's neighbours, but from those who have known one from infancy. It is no good here for me to pretend to be anything which I am not. If I were to pretend here to have greater abilities than I have you would soon find me out, and if I pretended, as I may have done in the course of my career, that I was more simple than I really am, then again you would know exactly how far I was deviating from the strict letter of the truth. I think it is good sometimes that one should come back into that atmosphere and environment.

I think it is also a good thing that the outside

14

world should know one or two things about Stourport, known well to us, but known very little to
them. How many people in London, where they
know so much, realize that Stourport was lighted
with gas before the City of London was ? Indeed,
had it not been for the railways—and as an old Tory
I am against all that kind of progress—Stourport
would have been a very large town by now. We
were essentially a creation of those days when people
looked to the canals as being the principal method
of England's navigation, and for that purpose the
site of this town was chosen, I think, with uncommon
skill : and, if indeed it be a desirable thing, of which
I am not convinced, to grow to be a big town, we
missed our chance in the early days of the railways,
when the main lines running through the country
passed this district by.

Stourport has the inestimable advantage of doing
its work in rural surroundings. If there is anything
—I will not say that has made me fit to succeed,
because whether success or not will attend me I cannot tell, and any way it does not very much matter if
one does one's best honestly—it is my training, which
has given me, whether I can use it or not, a knowledge
and a sympathy very difficult for any man to attain
who has had an exclusively political training. I regard
it as of the greatest value to myself that during the
formative years of my life, and during the ten and
twenty years when I first started work in the world,
I worked in close contact with all classes of people

in this country, and enjoyed, through no credit to myself, the goodwill which I have inherited from generations that have gone before me and left behind a name for honesty, fair play, right judgment, and kindliness to those with whom they worked. Through that, whether I succeed or not, I believe I have an understanding of the mind of the people of the country which I could have gained in no other way. It is through this that I have that ineradicable belief and faith in our people which sustains me through good times and evil, and it is because of this that I have every confidence that, whatever troubles may come to this country, or in this country at any time, the native strength and virtue of our people will overcome everything. There is only one thing which I feel is worth giving one's whole strength to, and that is the binding together of all classes of our people in an effort to make life in this country better in every sense of the word. That is the main end and object of my life in politics.

WORCESTER MEMORIES

AT WORCESTER

7th November, 1923

THIS is the second ceremony of the kind which I have attended within a short space of time, each of them of the greatest interest and honour. For any Englishman to receive the Freedom of the City of London is looked upon as one of the greatest tributes which can be paid to a man for his work ; but to receive a similar tribute in one's own home county touches the heart far more, and is an honour that, perhaps, in some ways is more highly appreciated than any honour that can possibly fall to one at any time, because it is a message of sympathy and encouragement from all those who know you best, from those amongst whom you sprang and were reared, those who know you and whence you came, what you have done, all your faults and your few virtues ; and yet in spite of that they combine to do this thing, and the feeling with which it is done, the unanimity, the appreciation, the goodwill, are exactly the kind of encouragement that a man needs when he has to perform such a task as mine.

As a Worcestershire man, and standing in the

heart of the city of Worcester, it is very natural that one's thoughts should go back to many things—to the rock from which you were hewn, the pit from whence you were digged ; and one thinks of those who went before one, whose work has contributed to make one's own life task possible. One thinks of those of one's ancestors, who left their old home in Shropshire about 150 years ago to seek their fortunes four miles inside this county at a little place that was then growing up, where Brindley had brought his new canal into Severn. One knows the struggles that they had in those days, and one knows the hard work and the careful thought and the thrift and the human kindliness that went on from generation to generation. It is interesting to remember the connection, which has lasted for about 120 years, between my own family and the old bank in Worcester. It was from the old bank 120 years ago that we raised with infinite difficulty £500. It was the old bank that helped to carry us through the crisis in the 'twenties of the last century, and much credit is due to them for having survived a period which brought down so many of the private banks throughout the kingdom. Time and time again did they stand our friends in days when we were less able to stand on our own feet than we are now, and I shall never forget it.

Having been, as it were, an emigrant from another county into Worcestershire, and having become Worcestershire by adoption, and finally Worcestershire by birth and ties for so many years, one knows in one's bones now that one is a Worcestershire man, and that there is nothing like it.   One came out of this red soil, and one will return to it and lay one's bones in it, and there is no soil like it in this country. It is remembering all these things, these innumerable ties that bind one to the city and the county, that makes a ceremony of this nature so touching at a time like this.

I am just one of yourselves, who has been called to special work for the country at this time.   I never sought the office.   I never planned out or schemed my life.   I have but one idea, which was an idea that I inherited, and it was the idea of service— service to the people of this country.   My father lived in that belief all his life, and behind him members of my family, in an obviously more restricted way, practised the same thing.   It is a tradition ; it is in our bones ; and we have to do it. That service seemed to lead one by way of business and the county council into Parliament, and it has led one through various strange paths to where one is ; but the ideal remains the same, because all my life I believed from my heart the words of Browning, " All service ranks the same with God."   It makes very little difference whether a man is driving a tramcar or sweeping streets or being Prime Minister, if he only brings to that service everything that is in him and performs it for the sake of mankind.

It is natural, perhaps, quite apart from one's

parentage, that one should feel this, because I lived as a child in the heart of Worcestershire, by the side of one of the last of the iron forges that were left in the rural districts of England, and the impressions of childhood are those that last, and as you get older come back more strongly.   Among the chief friends that I had in those days—they represented two sides of life, the industrial and the agricultural—one was a shepherd who could neither read nor write, but like many men of those days who could neither read nor write, he was a great deal more intelligent than many who can do both now.   He had a face like an old pippin, and he talked the undiluted tongue of our fathers.   I learned much from him.   Another man that I learned much from was one who had been a workman, and who rose to be a manager, and who went to work at ten years old on a twelve-hours' night-shift, thus being a link with an industrial past which, thank God, has passed away for ever.   But with such friends of one's childhood, it is little wonder that one learned a profound sympathy with and affection for the common man, of whom I am one, which has never deserted me and never will.

I learned instinctively and unconsciously another very useful lesson, and that is that a man is a gentleman by what comes from within, and I have known many in my life in all walks.   I do not want to go on " reminiscing," easy as it is, but I did want to say these few things to you, because if you do not scheme and plan your life, and if you leave it perhaps in higher hands than yours, and you look back, you will see how wonderfully the little things which you never noticed at the time all seem to fit into the ultimate scheme, and that the preparation for life which you have had, which you did not understand at the time, turns out to have been the very best preparation that you could have had. I am quite sure that that intimate knowledge that I had of working people, both industrial and rural, when I was a boy, has stood me in extraordinarily good stead in the last two or three years, because that natural sympathy that I had as a child, that came from acquaintance and friendship, has so ripened that one feels when one is giving one's life in service for the people of this country one is not working for any kind of abstraction or any large party of voters, but for the human men and women who are carrying on the daily toil of the world, with whom one has worked oneself and whom one has known on terms of intimacy. It is a great strength and a great help.

ON PEACE IN INDUSTRY

PEACE IN INDUSTRY. I

AT BIRMINGHAM
5th March, 1925

HOWEVER hardened a public speaker may be, and in however many places he may have spoken, he cannot rise for the first time in Birmingham Town Hall before a Birmingham audience without feeling a thrill of emotion. For a generation this great hall was associated throughout England with the names of two of our greatest orators—John Bright and Joseph Chamberlain.

Though we who are called, so far as we are able, to fill their places in the struggle to-day, may fall far short of them in eloquence, we can at least be stimulated by their example, so that we do not fall short of them in sincerity of purpose and in truth, and in an honest endeavour to improve the condition of our people.

To-night I have no desire to ask you to join with me in a pæan of victory. You and I are thankful for the decision to which the country came at the beginning of the winter, but we want to look forward now and to devote a short time to-night to looking at some of the problems which lie before us, to see what progress has been made, and to see in what direction the people of England should look for their own security.

I think we can best preface such an investigation by casting our eyes for a few moments at the continent of Europe, a continent separated from us indeed by a narrow strip of ocean, but joined to us by a hundred links of commerce and of humanity, indissolubly bound up with our fate, whether we like it or whether we do not. I think we may fairly claim that although there is much to be done in Europe, yet there are signs to-day of what has not been seen hitherto, and that is a general desire for stability, and what proceeds from desire, and is more important, the will to achieve stability.

It is only determination that will produce it, and until you have stability you can have no confidence, and until you have confidence you can never get that increased productive power which is one of the absolute necessities for the bettering of our own trade in England.

Now, not long ago Austria, for example, was on the verge of bankruptcy. Her administrative expenses were all in arrear; her industries were paralysed. Largely owing to the action of the League of Nations, and largely owing to the action of her own countrymen, she has been saved, and she has been put in a path, strait, indeed, but one which is leading her, and will lead her, into a position where once more she can make her contribution to the well-being of Europe, instead of being a black spot from which might spread the seeds of disease into other countries.

The same with Hungary—the same process, the same contribution, and the same results. And we see the new states brought into being since the War —Poland, Czecho-Slovakia, Jugo-Slavia—slowly, but surely, establishing their industries, buying raw material, which is the beginning, coming once more into the comity of industrial and commercial nations, and helping to start again that wheel of the circulation of industrial life which alone can bring health to Europe, and, by bringing health to Europe, health to us.

And in France, and in Belgium, there is a healthy and progressive increase in the industrial life of those countries, and bit by bit over the three years you have seen the healthy spots forming in Europe and spreading outwards, and gradually driving back the unhealthy parts, so that we are beginning to have a hope that before too long the body itself may be whole.

And Germany! The Dawes plan, which has settled—at any rate on paper—the reparations question has by that very factor increased confidence in the public finance of Germany, which means confidence in the public finance of that vast population of Central Europe. The fact that a successful loan was issued, that the Reichsbank has been reconstituted, and that the currency has been restored, has enabled private credits once more to function in Germany. The negotiation of a commercial treaty with this country means that if she will now play the game, there is no reason why the interrupted trade with Central Europe should not commence again to join in the increase of European and world trade for the ultimate betterment of everybody.

Her internal troubles are diminishing. We in England have, in the last year or two, made once more foreign loans to help to repair the shattered edifices throughout the world, and the United States has come in with loans, contrary to her usual practice, in Europe, to set in motion the creative energies of the peoples, which energies will be gradually reflected in the growing purchasing powers of the peoples.

The failure of that purchasing power and the financial chaos which followed on the War have been, I was going to say amongst, but I would say the chief reason for that appalling depression from which we are only just beginning to emerge in this country.

But what is it that has prevented the recovery of Europe proceeding at a greater speed than it has, and what is it to-day that is the one check and the one blight on an outlook which is beginning to look more hopeful ? It is that cursed and diabolic suspicion between man and man and nation and nation that robs Europe of that sense of security that is essential to the unity of spirit which we must have before the world can function aright.

It is to help to abolish that suspicion, to help to show the better way, that Mr. Austen Chamberlain leaves England to-morrow to see what he can accomplish amongst the nations of Europe. It is his attempt to execute that great mission that has prevented him from having the pleasure of being here to-night, and has prevented you from having the pleasure of giving him the welcome he so well deserves in Birmingham. There is no member of the Government who has a more arduous task than he ; there is no one better qualified by training and by temperament at this time to make a success of that mission.

Now, having said a few words about Europe, let us look nearer home. There is much the same story to be told—a story of constant struggle, and, on the whole, a story of ground gained and hope for the future.

But while in England we can put our finger here and there on the hopeful signs, there are many that cause us anxiety. We have only a very partial prosperity, an industry here and there, sometimes one, sometimes another ; but for four years we have hoped against hope that we might be able to show prosperity in all our industries.

Two years ago the coal industry enjoyed a brief spell of prosperity, due partly to the conditions in the Ruhr ; and in the wake of the coal trade followed

the trades in iron and steel.   But, as prospects in the
Ruhr looked better, and greater prosperity seemed
in store for them, so the temporary improvement
here gave way to depression.   As those industries
tailed off, there has been improvement in cotton,
there has been fairly good trade in the electrical
industry ; but we are denied still that all-round and
simultaneous improvement which is necessary before
we can feel ourselves in that position of security
and stability which we all desire to see.

If we look at the figures of our foreign trade as a
whole, we do indeed find some ground for moderate
hopefulness. We find that the balance of imports
over exports is not larger proportionately than we
are accustomed to, and that our invisible exports
come to our rescue as they did before the War, and
we cannot yet say that we have an adverse balance.

But whatever conclusions people may draw from
the examination of figures of exports and imports,
I never can help translating this story into terms of
unemployment. At the end of January there were
a million and a quarter on the registers—practically
the same as a year ago—no real substantial improvement.

Now, you know well enough in Birmingham how
the steel and heavy engineering trades, and you
know well enough by repute how the shipbuilding
trades, are suffering to-day. These heavy trades
have in their numbers something like 10 per cent. of
the insured population of this country, but among

these trades to-day their unemployment represents more than 20 per cent. of the total unemployment. They are trades closely interlocked, and they are trades closely dependent and immediately reacting on the coal trade ; and I think I ought to say a word or two on the subject of this trade.

The production of coal in Europe last year increased by scores of millions of tons at a time when there was a heavy under-consumption of coal compared with the pre-war standard. It is not surprising in these circumstances that our export of coal dropped by 18 million tons. The increased cost of production here wiped out all that margin of profit at which some of the older and less efficient pits worked.

And you find pits closed, especially in the North of England and in North and South Wales ; and here and there, the unexampled spectacle of pools of unemployed labour in the mining industry, where they have little immediate prospect of a resumption of work.

Now, the iron and steel trades have been specially hit by the condition of the shipbuilding trade. There you have fewer ships being built ; you have an intensively increased foreign competition, and you have at home an immensely increased capacity in point of output and a largely increased technical capacity ; and you have at places like Sheffield and Barrow, where there were enormous accumulations of labour during the War for special purposes, the almost impossible task of finding in works of peace sufficient employment to take over not only their old population but the men who were attracted there for munition work in time of war.

And so it is, seven years nearly after the War, that we yet see this prolonged and intensified depression, and this horrible figure of unemployment.

Now, if you look back you will find that in 1908 you had very nearly as bad a time of unemployment, and you had it in those industries of which I have just spoken to you.

But what is the difference ? In 1908 it was of comparatively short duration. To-day, we have lived through four years of it, and who can say whether we are yet at the end ? There are, of course, international factors largely beyond our power to deal with, but there are national factors within our own control. We stand to-day at a point where, roughly speaking, one out of every ten of the insured population is out of work—a thought sufficient to arrest the imagination of the dullest and the most thoughtless amongst us—and a challenge to all of us to use every power we have to remedy this state of things. But there is no direct remedy from the State alone. There can be no direct remedy by private men alone.

Nothing can be done unless we can all pull together with a will. And I am—and I speak seriously—quite profoundly thankful that the Labour Party have been in office, and for this reason : that they now know that they, no more than any other

Government, have been able to produce a panacea that would remedy unemployment. And in their hearts they must admit that they have no remedy which can be guaranteed to cure this disease and at the same time maintain unimpaired the international position and power of the British Empire.

And it is at this moment, with one in ten of the working population unemployed, at this moment when in some industries there is a faint hope of a revival, at this moment when other industries, with the utmost endeavours on their part, can but just hold their own, that we witness in England signs of an industrial storm gathering, which, if it were to break, would spread misery far and wide, and sweep back, possibly for years, all chance of returning and reviving prosperity.

By the natural evolution of our industrial life in England we are confronted to-day, and shall be more and more, with great consolidations of capital managed by small concentrated groups, and by great organisations of Labour led by experienced and responsible leaders. That position must be accepted. It is the natural accompaniment of the large-scale production which is gradually becoming the pre-dominant force in all the industrial countries of the world.

It is perfectly true that if the great trade unions of this country, such as the miners, the transport workers, and the railwaymen, unite on a policy of trying to enforce a demand for higher wages in their own trades by means of a strike, they have it in their power to hold up at the same time many industries in this country, and do them irreparable damage.

Now, I said when I concluded what I had to say about the state of affairs on the Continent of Europe, there was one element that must be removed before you could get stability, before you could get security, and before you could get what follows on security—disarmament. That was suspicion, and suspicion must be removed.

I am whole-heartedly with those men who talk about disarmament on the Continent, peace on the Continent, and the removal of suspicion on the Continent, but far more do I plead for disarmament at home, and for the removal of that suspicion at home that tends to poison the relations of man and man, the removal of which alone can lead us to stability for our struggling industry, and create the confidence in which our people may be able to move forward to better things.

By all means let us aim at having our conferences abroad for these good ends. Let us not neglect to have these conferences at home for these good ends, which touch us far more closely and far more nearly than anything which happens across the Channel.

Why must we reserve all our talk of peace and our prayers for peace for the Continent, and forget to have our talks and our prayers for peace at home ? It is one of the paradoxes of public life that from the very lips which preach pacifism abroad we hear the cries for war at home. Who was it said of Rousseau that he was a lover of his kind, but a hater of his kin ? The children of such a philosophy can only bring damnation to this country.

Having said that, I want to recognise, in the most generous way that I can, that there have been speeches made amongst the leaders of Labour to-day which would endorse every word that I have uttered ; and I recognise the courage of those speeches, because the men who uttered them are trying at the same time to do their duty to those whom they represent and to that greater community, their country.

When a man is in public life, whether he be a Labour leader or the leader of the Tory Party, if he speaks the truth that is in him and that he burns to tell, often enough he will find many who will be ready to deride him for what he has said. I want to endorse the kind of speeches to which I have referred.

I want to plead for a truce.

In the Middle Ages, when the whole of Europe was in conflict, one part with another and one fragment with another, men of goodwill strove in vain to get what they called a truce of God, in which people might compose their differences and live like brothers.

I want a truce of God in this country, that we may compose our differences, that we may join all our strengths together to see if we cannot pull the country into a better and happier condition.

It is little that a Government can do; these reforms, these revolutions must come from the people themselves.

The organisations of employers and men, if they take their coats off to it, are far more able to work out the solutions of their troubles than the politicians. Let them put the State out of their minds and get down to it, as the Foreign Secretary is getting down to it to-day to try to improve the relations of foreign countries by seeking peace and pursuing it through every corner and alley that he may. So let those who represent labour and capital get down to it, and seek and pursue peace through every alley and every corner of this country.

And just as those who want peace in Europe have ever before their minds, if they fail in their object, what war may mean to the Continent, so let those who are working for peace in England realise that the breach of the peace in industry can mean nothing more than the prolongation of what is already too much misery among those who are suffering from unemployment to-day.

Indeed, how much there is for those responsible for the conduct of the industry—and I mean masters and men just the same—how much there is for them to-day to try to discover, and to try to understand.

Let me give one illustration. I have a letter before me now from a British firm which has works in this country, works in France, and works in Germany. And the making of a machine of exactly similar type costs £565 here, in Germany £520, and in France £400. Now all those concerned in industry should try to get at the root of the reason why a thing of this kind is possible.

Look for a moment at the employers' side.

Are the reasons for our failure to compete connected with over-capitalisation, are they connected with defective management, with wasteful use of plant and of material ?

Are they due at all to the absence of facilities for economic marketing ?

Are State subsidies granted on the Continent ?

Is there a freer use abroad of unskilled labour in various processes ?

What is the cause ?

And on the men's side, should not they look into the question of whether in the allocation to different branches of labour, there is not greater fluidity and absence of demarcation disputes which make it easier for the Continent to compete ?

These are questions no Government can settle, that no Government can interfere with, and no Government can solve ; but to get a correct answer is life and death to those in industry, whether they be employers or employed.

These are the kinds of issues that want to be examined by both parties round a table, and to be approached, not with a view on the one side to get an increase of wages, or with a view on the other to get a reduction of wages, but to get at the reasons and

see where the fault lies. All should take counsel together and see where and how improvement can be
made in this country to achieve the desired result.

And there should be an end once and for all of
that secretiveness in business which has so often
poisoned the atmosphere by causing suspicion.

When you discuss disarmament there must be all
the cards on the table. Is not mystery of any kind
the mother of suspicion? Confidence breeds confidence, and I would give it in the fullest and largest
degree.

I would like to see firms who have factories as I
have described, place on the table carefully prepared
analyses of the comparative costs in the different
countries for the men to examine, for accountants to
examine—no mystery, no secretiveness, but a common
desire to get at facts, and a common desire to help.

I do not pretend for a moment that all is easy if
you simply gather men around the table. There
are differences—differences of education, of early
environment, psychological differences, differences
of training. I was struck once by a remark made,
I think it was, by Mr. Hodges in stating the miners'
case in the recent coal dispute, that he never felt less
nervous than in presenting it at No. 10 Downing Street,
to members of a Government which he had no reason
to believe was particularly anxious to agree with him.

I understand what he meant, and it has often
struck me that it might be of real help to conferences
in trades between the employers and the employed

if they were presided over by a neutral person, a man qualified by his own character and ability, by his detached and independent outlook, and by the confidence which people felt in his fairmindedness— that the presence of such a chairman might enable two parties to get on with greater ease, with greater freedom, and with more success in ultimate results.

There are other things arising to which our leaders of industry, whether they be from the ranks of the employers, or from the ranks of the men, must devote their attention at this present day, if they do not wish to make confusion still worse confounded.

It is not wages alone that have to be studied, and that we must keep our eyes on. If you fix on paper minimum standards of pay it does not follow that those standards will, in fact, apply to all the men in the industry. What often results is the stoppage of the marginal factory or the marginal coal-pit, or you may find that some of them near the margin will have to go on short time, and you often find that many men are thrown out of employment.

In the same way you often hear men's leaders to-day speaking about the necessity for rigorous efficiency on the part of employers, but rigorous efficiency again often acts hardly on many of those employed. You have to take the long view as well as the short ; and I think in these days what those most concerned in industry have to study is what can be accomplished in the way of insurance benefit, and what burdens can be borne by industry—this in consultation with the Government—and how far regulations and rules made in trade unions to fit circumstances of many years ago are fitted to meet the circumstances not only of to-day, but the circumstances that lie ahead of us.

Here, again, there is ample room, ample scope, for such conferences as I have advocated, and, mind you, for the very best brains and the best hearts that the best men among the employers and the men themselves can put forward. This is not work for hacks, it is work for the statesmen among us.

I don't know whether things may be different and happier in Russia, for I have not had the advantage of having six weeks in that country. But in England let us never forget this : that under our system trade expansion depends so much on initiative and enterprise, and on the willingness of our people—men and women—to embark their savings in industry in anticipation of making something rather more out of industry than they could make if the savings were kept in a stocking.

Now, the element of risk and uncertainty cannot be absent from industry—it is inseparable from our system of production—but readiness to embark on that form of investment is a question of confidence. Nothing can destroy that confidence more surely than what destroys confidence on the Continent— no sense of security. The present unsettlement in this country is in itself a clog on the wheels of progress.

There may be a better industrial system imaginable than ours, and I hope indeed we may be slowly moving towards something better ; but there is no doubt in my mind that if it were possible to destroy the present system in a moment, those who destroyed it would cause a shipwreck, and they would not bring into being a ship in which to take away the survivors.

Short, too, of any deliberate destruction of our industry, such as we have seen advocated in a few quarters, I dread that subtle poison of hatred which is being preached in some quarters, which weakens the faith of men in their own efficient service and sound workmanship—the very things which have built up the reputation of our great country, on which we still live. You may have one of the finest fleets of liners in this world, you may have it owned by the State, and you may have it run by the State ; but if you have a crew bent on defying all that makes for co-operation and discipline you will bankrupt that fleet.

It has not come to that in this country, and in my belief it never will. The power of managing our own affairs in our own way is the greatest gift of Englishmen. We have demonstrated that fact in the past, and we shall demonstrate it in the future. It has been ours in a growing degree for a dozen centuries. And I cannot put that thought before you better than in the words of a distinguished Oxford man, the late Master of Balliol, who wrote :

" Nowhere was the village community so real and so enduring a thing as it was in England for at least twelve centuries of its history. In every parish men met almost daily in humble but very real self-government, to be judged by their fellows or fined by them, or punished as bad characters, to settle the ploughing times and harvest times, the fallowing and the grassing rules for the whole village. To these twelve centuries of discipline we owe the peculiar English capacity for self-government, the enormous English development of the voluntary principle in all manner of institutions (clubs, associations, hospitals, joint stock) and the aptitude for colonisation. Our politics, our commercial enterprise, our Colonial Empire, are all due to the spirit of co-operation, the spirit of fair play, and ' give and take,' the habit of working to a common purpose which tempered the hard and grim individuality of the national character."

And if I have a message to-night for you and the people of the country, it is just this. I would say :

" England ! Steady ! Look where you are going ! Human hands were given us to clasp, and not to be raised against one another in fratricidal strife."

PEACE IN INDUSTRY. II

In the House of Commons, on the Second Reading of the Trade Union (Political Fund) Bill.

6th March, 1925

In some ways this is a very difficult speech for me to make. The matter of the Bill itself digs right into one of the most difficult and fundamental questions in the country to-day, and it touches at various points questions which have interested me during the whole of my working life. I have thought so much about them, and I feel that I have so much to say about them, that my difficulty will be in choosing the little that I can possibly say to-day and finding words to express clearly to the House what is in my mind.

I often wonder if all the people in this country realise the inevitable changes that are coming over the industrial system in England. People are apt either to get their knowledge of the industrial system from textbooks, which must be half a generation behind, or from some circumstance familiar to them at a fixed and static point in their lives, whereas, as a matter of fact, ever since the industrial system began in this country, it has been not only in a state of evolution, but in a state of evolution that, I think, historians in the centuries to come, when they write its history, will acknowledge to be an evolution that has developed at a far more rapid rate than was visible to the people who lived in these times.

I hope the House will bear with me and forgive me if I draw for a few minutes on my own experience, because it so happens that, owing to the peculiar circumstances of my own life, I have seen a great deal of this evolution taking place before my own eyes.

I worked for many years in an industrial business, and I had under me a large number, or what was then a large number, of men. And it so happened, as this was an old family business, with an old and, I venture to say, very good tradition, that when I was first in business I was probably working under a system that was already passing. I doubt if its like could have been found in any of the big, modern industrial towns of this country, even at that time.

It was a place where I knew, and had known from childhood, every man on the ground ; a place where I was able to talk with the men not only about the troubles in the works, but troubles at home and their wives. It was a place where strikes and lock-outs were unknown. It was a place where the fathers and grandfathers of the men then working there had worked, and where their sons went automatically into the business. It was also a place where nobody ever " got the sack," and where we had a natural sympathy for those who were less concerned in efficiency than is this generation, and where a large number of old gentlemen used to spend their days sitting on the handles of wheelbarrows, smoking their pipes.

Oddly enough, it was not an inefficient community. It was the last survival of that type of works which ultimately became swallowed up in one of those great combinations towards which the industries of to-day are tending.

I remember very well the impact of the outside world that came on us, that showed how industry was changing in this country. Nothing had interrupted the even tenor of our ways for many years, until one day there came a great strike in the coalfields ; it was one of the earlier strikes, and it became a national strike.

We tried to carry on as long as we could, but, of course, it became more and more difficult to carry on, and gradually furnace after furnace was damped down and the chimneys ceased to smoke, and about 1,000 men, who had no interest in the dispute that was going on, were thrown out of work, through no fault of their own, at a time when there was no unemployment benefit.

I confess that that event set me thinking very hard.

It seemed to me at that time a monstrous injustice to these men, because I looked upon them as my own family, and it hit me very hard—I would not have mentioned this, only it got into the Press two or three years ago—and I made an allowance to them, not a large one, but something, for six weeks to carry them along, because I felt they were being so unfairly treated.

But there was more in it really than that. There was no conscious unfair treatment of these men by the masters. It simply was that we were gradually passing into a new state of industry when the small firms and the small industries were being squeezed out, and business was all tending towards great amalgamations, on the one side of employers, and on the other side of the men, and when we came in any form between these two forces, God help those who stood outside !

That has been the tendency of industry. There is nothing that could change it, because it comes largely, if not principally, from that driving force of necessity in the world that makes people combine together for competition and for the protection they need against that competition.

Those two forces with which we have to reckon are enormously strong, and they are the two forces in this country to which now to a great extent, and it will be a greater extent in the future, we are committed. We have to see what wise statesmanship can do to steer the country through this time of evolution until we can get to the next stage of our industrial civilisation.

It is obvious from what I have said that the organisations of both masters and men—or, if you like the more modern phrase invented by economists,

who always invent beastly words, employers and
employees—these organisations throw an immense
responsibility on the organisations themselves and
on those who elect them, and, although big men have
been thrown up on both sides, there are a great many
on both sides who have not got the requisite qualities
of head and heart for business.

There are many men with good heads and no
hearts, and many men with good hearts and no heads.

What the country wants to-day from the men who
sit on this side of the House and on that is to exercise
the same care as the men who have to conduct those
great organisations from inside.

I should like to try to clear our minds of cant on
this subject, and recognise that the growth of these
associations is not necessarily a bad thing in itself,
but that, whatever associations may call themselves,
it is the same human nature in both, and exactly the
same problems have to be met, although we hear a
good deal more of some of those problems than of
others.

Now, if you look at an employers' organisation for
a moment—and we will assume that it has come into
being to protect the industry in the world market—
we cannot lose sight of the fact that in that organisation, just as much as in the men's organisation, the
mere fact of organising involves a certain amount of
sacrifice of personal liberty. That cannot be helped.
Everybody knows that perfectly well, both employers
and employees.

To a certain extent both these organisations must on one side be uneconomic.

A trade union is uneconomic in one sense of the word when it restricts output and when it levels down the work to a lower level. It is an association for the protection of the weaker men which has often proved uneconomic.

Exactly the same thing happens in the employers' organisation.

Primarily, it is protective, but in effect it is very often uneconomic, because it keeps in existence works which, if left to the process of competition, would be squeezed out, and whose prolonged existence is really only a weakness to the country.

Also it has another very curious effect, not at all dissimilar from that of the trade union reaction which shows that both those organisations are instinct with English traditions. The workmen's organisation is formed to see that under the conditions a workman cannot get his living in a particular trade unless he belongs to that union. An employers' organisation is formed in that particular trade for the protection of the trade, and it has the result of effectively preventing any new man starting in that trade.

In this great problem which is facing the country in years to come, it may be from one side or the other that disaster may come, but surely it is plain that the only progress that can be obtained in this country is by those two bodies of men—so similar in their strength and so similar in their weaknesses—learning to understand each other and not to fight each other.

It is perfectly true that trade unionism has its weak spots. We are primarily discussing trade unions, and that is why I shall content myself to speak about trade unions only. It is perfectly true that my hon. and learned Friends [Mr. Macquisten and Mr. Greaves-Lord, who moved and seconded the Second Reading of the Bill] have laid their finger on three points which trade unionists themselves know are their weak spots. That can be seen by the interruptions that came from the Labour benches.

Those three points are, the question whether in all cases the subject of the levy is treated fairly, the question of the ballot, and the question of book-keeping. To my mind it is impossible to dissociate one of these questions from the other, and they really all hang together.

The whole tradition of our country has been to let Englishmen develop their own associations in their own way, and with that I agree. But there are limits to that. I spoke a little earlier—and I spoke with a purpose—about the recognition of the change in the industrial situation in those works with which I was connected, when for the first time what was done in the way of organising the coal strike suddenly came and hit thousands of men who had nothing to do with it and had no direct interest in it.

As these associations come along and become more powerful, on whichever side they are, there may come a time when not only may they injure their own members—about which probably there would be a good deal of argument—but when they may directly injure the State. It is at that moment that any Government should say that, whatever freedom and latitude in that field may be left to any kind of association in this free country, nothing shall be done that shall injure the State, which is the concern of all of us and far greater than all of us or our interests.

I have not very much more to say. I have just tried to put, as clearly as I can in a few words, my conviction that we are moving forward rapidly from an old state of industry into a newer, and the question is : What is that newer state going to be ?

No man, of course, can say what form evolution is taking. Of this, however, I am quite sure, that whatever form we may see, possibly within this generation, or at any rate in the time of the next generation, it has got to be a form of close partnership, however that is going to be arrived at ; and it will not be a partnership the terms of which will be laid down, at any rate not yet, in Acts of Parliament, or from this Party or that.

It has got to be a partnership of men who understand their own work, and it is little help that they can get really either from politicians or from intellectuals.

There are few men fitted to judge of and to settle and to arrange the problem that distracts the country to-day between employers and employed.

There are few men qualified to intervene who have not themselves been right through the mill.

I always want to see, at the head of these organisations on both sides, men who have been right through the mill, and who themselves know exactly where the shoe pinches, and who know exactly what can be conceded and what cannot, and who can make their reasons plain ; and I hope that we shall always find such men trying to steer their respective ships side by side, instead of making for head-on collisions.

Having said what I have said about that, what am I to say about the attitude of the Party of which I have the honour to be the head ?

I do not know whether the House will forgive me if I speak for a minute or two on a rather personal note.

For two years past, in the face of great difficulties, perhaps greater than many were aware of, I have striven to consolidate, and to breathe a living force into my great Party. Friends of mine who have done me the honour to read my speeches during that time have seen clearly, however ill they may have been expressed, the ideals at which I have been aiming.

I spoke on that subject again last night at Birmingham, and I shall continue to speak on it as long as I am where I am.

We find ourselves, after these two years, in power, in possession of perhaps the greatest majority our Party has ever had, and with the general assent of the country. Now how did we get there? It was not by promising to bring this Bill in; it was because, rightly or wrongly, we succeeded in creating an impression throughout the country that we stood for stable Government and for peace in the country between all classes of the community.

Those were the principles for which we fought; those were the principles on which we won; and our victory was not won entirely by the votes of our own Party, splendidly as they fought. I should think that the number of Liberals who voted for us at the last Election ran into six figures, and I should think that we probably polled more Labour votes than were polled on the other side.

That being so, what should our course be at the beginning of a new Parliament? I have not myself the slightest doubt. Last year the Leader of the Labour Party [Mr. Ramsay Macdonald], when he was Prime Minister, suspended what had been settled by the previous Government, and that was further progress for the time being on the scheme of Singapore. He did it on the ground that it was a gesture for peace, and he hoped that it would be taken as such by all the countries in the world. He hoped that a gesture of that kind might play its part in leading to what we all want to see, that is, a reduction in the world's armaments.

I want my Party to-day to make a gesture to the country of a similar nature, and to say to them : " We have our majority ; we believe in the justice of this Bill which has been brought in to-day, but we are going to withdraw our hand, and we are not going to push our political advantage home at a moment like this. Suspicion which has prevented stability in Europe is the one poison that is preventing stability at home, and we offer the country to-day this : We, at any rate, are not going to fire the first shot. We stand for peace. We stand for the removal of suspicion in the country. We want to create an atmosphere, a new atmosphere in a new Parliament for a new age, in which the people can come together. We abandon what we have laid our hands to. We know we may be called cowards for doing it. We know we may be told that we have gone back on our principles. But we believe we know what at this moment the country wants, and we believe it is for us in our strength to do what no other Party can do at this moment, and to say that we at any rate stand for peace."

I know, I am as confident as I can be of anything, that that will be the feeling of all those who sit behind me, and that they will accept the Amendment which I have put down in the spirit in which I have moved it. And I have equal confidence in my fellow-countrymen throughout the whole of Great Britain.

Although I know that there are those who work for different ends from most of us in this House, yet there are many in all ranks and all parties who will re-echo my prayer :

" *Give peace in our time, O Lord.*"

INDUSTRY AND PSYCHOLOGY

AT THE NATIONAL INSTITUTE OF INDUSTRIAL PSYCHOLOGY

12th November, 1925

WE are met to-night to celebrate the invasion of the realm of industry by psychology. We have all of us been familiar for many years past with the study that economists have made of industry and the study that moralists have made of the development of the personality of the individual ; but the systematic study of industrial society by psychologists is a matter, as I understand, of the last three or four years. Certainly it is something quite new since I had the pleasure of being in business.

Within the present century there has been a drastic overhauling of a great many of the assumptions with which some of us were familiar in our youth, whether the assumptions were those of the economists, the moralists, or of the psychologists. Psychology has been applied not only to the handling of the individual, but to individuals in groups, or in the mass, in association. The results of this change in the line of investigation are now just beginning to penetrate our economic thinking. The Institute, to

celebrate which we are here to-night, is a striking
example of this change, and it has had from its start
the support of two men whom I am proud to think
I may call my friends—Lord Balfour and Lord
Haldane. It has also enlisted the support of
employers and employed.

There exists a certain interesting and harmonious
relation between this voluntary body and one that
has been set up by the Government—the Industrial
Fatigue Research Board, which works as a branch
of the Medical Research Council. Roughly speaking, the Industrial Fatigue Board initiates work and
undertakes experiments which are likely to have
fruitful results and be of interest, though un-
remunerative in themselves. Your Institute spends
private money, and it obtains support from among
those who stand to benefit by the results of your
investigations, but who are undoubtedly attracted to
the work of the Institute through the interest which
they take in the problems you are attacking. The
Institute, so far as I have been able to learn, is sur-
veying the vast realm covered by the operation of
the Factory Acts, and it is striving to introduce into
that realm improvements—not improvements which
require legislation, but improvements in mental and
bodily conditions of work. The study of such
things as lighting, heating, ventilation, movement of
the body, cultivation of interest, the avoidance of
fatigue, occupational guidance—in other words, the
study of the whole human factor in relation to the

machine and the job—that, as I understand it, is the field of study of the industrial psychologist.

A movement of this kind has this in common with the League of Nations : it has two principal obstacles to encounter—the prejudice of people who think it can do nothing, and the support of people who think it can do everything. In the first place it met, not unnaturally, with the resistance of those who thought that, in spite of its name, it was another capitalist dodge to rivet the chains of the wage slave more firmly than before. I think it is now clear, not only among the leaders of the employers and among the leaders of the men, but also among the men themselves, that in this Institute they have a real friend.

The fundamental question is how to make the most of the individual, with all his idiosyncrasies, in his work. If you consider the matter in the realm of sport, there seems really much less to wonder at in the work of the Institute than if you regarded it in the realm in which they are now working. Consider what is meant by training for a boat race. It means nothing more nor less than true co-operation of effort, rhythmic movement, distribution of energy in the proper place, and at the right time, with the minimum fatigue and the elimination of wasted effort. That is all. And there you have a very suggestive parallel with industry. It is quite true that the changes which accompanied the Industrial Revolution have been far more costly in human life and human wear and tear than they would have been had our ancestors been as wise as we sometimes think that we ourselves are. But these depressing features of the Industrial Revolution, whatever they have brought in their train inside workshops, have had a tendency to bring in their train outside workshops one very bad thing, and that is a dislike of work itself. If work can be presented in a palatable form, I am not sure that the ordinary human being does not like it, provided that he gets a reasonable amount of play. The real enemies are overwork, under-payment, insecurity and bad conditions. These are the real evils, to the assuaging of which the work of this Institute, as I understand it, is directed, and in that we wish more power to its elbow.

We must not exaggerate what is possible. You cannot abolish repetitive work ; you cannot, even in a Socialist State ; and, after all, the monotony of the workman's life is very much due to the monotony of the consumers' demands. If a man wants the same thing every day, the man who provides it will have a monotonous task.

I am no mathematician, but I believe a straight line is, or was, the shortest way between two points, but I am told that curved movements are preferable to straight lines—whether on grounds of aesthetics or comfort I am not sure—and there is no doubt, as Mr. Myers has discovered, of the economic importance of rhythm, which has been gradually recognised in industry, I understand, and made use of. There must be something in rhythm which appeals to human nature. Witness the popularity at present of dancing, and witness also the vogue of the Volga Boat Song, which always makes me want to run along the bank and pull the barge.

Under the aegis of the Institute I am told that the miners, some of them, have been able to pick coal with greater regularity and have gained happiness thereby. That opens up a new field, and I am thinking seriously of asking Mr. Cook to bring in that which Mr. Thomas knows so well—that Welsh gift of music—and to set his men swinging their picks to the tune of " The Men of Harlech " or, better still, " The Rising of the Lark," and give us an output that will defy foreign competition.

But, seriously, if solutions can be found along these lines—if anything can cause the man, the woman, the boy and the girl at the heavy or monotonous job to find ways of doing that job with as great or with greater efficiency and with less strain, more comfort, more happiness—you will add more, perhaps, to a combination of human efficiency and human happiness than we politicians can hope to do by anything that lies in our power.

And there is another line on which you are working. You are always paying attention, I understand, to boys and girls who are leaving school in finding suitable occupations according to their fitness. This is a matter of tremendous importance, and involves practically what so many of us talk about—equality of opportunity. But I expect even this Institute has got a good deal to learn in that direction. One's first inclination is to smile at the idea of testing intelligence and vocational aptitude. I should be extraordinarily sorry at my age to have either of those things tested by anyone. We must not expect from this Institute infallible results, but I shall watch the results with intense interest, not only because I believe you may do a great work among the young people, but because I see an infinitely lighter task before my successor when he is able to apply the tests of this Institute to candidates for the Cabinet. If I can only draw on the resources of the psychologist to test the suitability of all candidates for Cabinet rank in initiative and self-control under criticism, intuitive insight into what Lancashire is going to say to-morrow, and when trade is going to revive, how much easier it would be ; and if we could only test also their physical qualifications for all-night sittings, and how long they can speak without boring an audience, then, indeed, Mr. Myers, you will rise up, and we shall call you blessed.

THE GOSPEL OF HATE

From a Speech in the House of Commons
16th February, 1923

ONE word about the speech delivered last night by
the hon. Member for Motherwell. (Mr. Newbold.)
I have always been a student of history, and I learned
from him several things that I had not known before.
There was only one remark of his on which I wish
to comment. He said that when the Labour Party
had been in power, and failed, he was coming in.
I believe that the hon. Member for Silvertown
(Mr. J. Jones) expressed dissent. I am myself of
that somewhat flabby nature that always prefers
agreement to disagreement, and I welcome the
opportunity of recording the fact that I find myself
in hearty and uncompromising agreement with the
hon. Member for Silvertown. When the Labour
Party sit on these benches, we shall all wish them
well in their effort to govern the country. But I am
quite certain that whether they succeed or fail there
will never in this country be a Communist Government, and for this reason, that no gospel founded on
hate will ever seize the hearts of our people—the
people of Great Britain. It is no good trying to cure
the world by spreading out oceans of bloodshed. It

59

is no good trying to cure the world by repeating that pentasyllabic French derivative, " Proletariat." The English language is the richest in the world in thought. The English language is the richest in the world in monosyllables. Four words, of one syllable each, are words which contain salvation for this country and for the whole world, and they are " Faith," " Hope," " Love," and " Work." No Government in this country to-day, which has not faith in the people, hope in the future, love for its fellow-men, and which will not work and work and work, will ever bring this country through into better days and better times, or will ever bring Europe through or the world through.

ON POLITICAL LIFE

SERVICE

AT THE LEEDS LUNCHEON CLUB
13th March, 1925

I WANT to begin by going back a few years and trying to voice to this room thoughts that perhaps have not been expressed in public, but which were common to a vast number of thinking men during the years of the war. I am one of those (of whom there are many here) who when the war broke out were too old for active service, but who were possessed in those days of the war with a consuming desire to do something for our country, and to look round to find where we could most usefully give service.

I think probably everybody here, members of such a club as yours, found their vocation at that time. But as the war went on, the effect of it psychologically was curious. Many of the things that had played a large part in our lives before shrank into insignificance, and we felt that the world could never be the same again to us who had grown to maturity in the years of peace. I think some of us found that we were getting to cling much more loosely to material wealth, and to realise that wealth was made to be a servant and not a master—that as a servant it had a most useful function to perform, that as a master it meant damnation.

I think, too, we felt this : we were not peculiarly impressed with speeches that talked of the glorious time that was coming after the war. We realised what the war meant in the world. We felt the foundations of civilisation in Europe cracking. We knew as business men that for a generation this country and the world would be as a whole far, far poorer, and we realised early the struggle that must result to repair the cracks in the foundations of our civilisation and to restore to the country that level of prosperity which she had enjoyed before the war. I think, too, many of us had little faith in supermen. I think that our experience in business had taught us that, as a matter of fact, there are no such things as supermen, and that we should have to rely on the innate common-sense, integrity, courage and faith of the common men and women of this country if we were to make good.

I think probably those thoughts which I certainly had, and which, I gather, you had, were pretty common throughout the country. It was for that reason, feeling as I did, that I was driven into the course which I embraced in December, 1916, when I accepted Mr. Bonar Law's offer to serve as his Parliamentary Secretary. I did that deliberately, because I believed that at my time of life, having already sufficient means to be independent of the active business in which I had passed my life up to then, I had the opportunity of giving my services to the country without any feeling that it was necessary to be remunerated for them.

There is nothing singular in that. There must have been millions of men who felt as I did. I have never said, or believed, that that service which I had the opportunity of rendering was one whit higher or better than any other. All service ranks the same, according to the spirit in which it is performed.

One of the sources of the great strength of our country in every part of the kingdom is that there are men who have no personal ambition for themselves to get where the limelight is brightest and publicity is greatest. And as long as our country can go on producing that type, which I am thankful to say it is producing from all classes of the community—so long as that is the case, I should never despair of England.

There is another observation I would like to make about the war before I pass on. It became evident to me long before the war was over that the effect of it, which would hit this country hardest in the years immediately succeeding, was the tragedy of the loss of the men who were just qualifying and getting ready to be the leaders of our younger men—the men who had already been at work in the factory and the mill, in all kinds of business and in the professions, who were just beginning to be masters of their own work—men of about thirty years of age, who by now would have been qualified to be leaders in their respective spheres.

There is nothing in the first twenty years after the war that can make good to this country the loss of so many men of that age. And that was an additional reason why we men who were middle-aged already when the war began should have banded ourselves together by the time the war ended under a vow to our better selves that we would give for the rest of our lives, as a thank-offering to the dead, nothing but the best services we could render to our country. It has become our lot not to seek the ease that we might legitimately seek, but to carry on to the end and help the next generation that is coming along —the generation that was too young to fight—help that to take its place as and when the time comes. It is, and it will be, a tremendous burden on the older men, but it is their proud contribution—the giving of the best they can to help a broken and a shattered world.

Among the problems that we have to face to-day there are some with which you are peculiarly fitted to deal, and where your advice, knowledge, understanding and enthusiasm may be of the greatest service to your country. In few things is it more difficult to make sufficiently rapid progress than in the problem of housing, and that problem in the big towns and cities of our country is linked up with kindred and greater problems of the planning of our cities. I spoke last night (not for the first time) of the rapidity with which the change had transformed our country, the change wrought by the growth of our industrial system. It was so unexpected, so unforeseen, and so incalculable in its effects that men were unable, and they had not the imagination, to plan and to look forward. If they had only done so how much easier our task would have been ! But we to-day not only have to devote ourselves to undoing the evil effects of things left undone by those who went before us ; we in our time must look ahead to plan that we do not leave problems for our descendants as grave as have been left for us.

In the growth of our big industrial centres to-day let us, while there is yet time, look forward and plan to see where the factories of the future are to be, and where the houses of the future are to be, and where the open spaces and the playing fields are to be, and how people are to be got to and from their work— that complicated system of transport. All these things need thought, sympathy, imagination and vision. In a gathering like this there are men who are capable of doing most useful work of this kind.

One centre after another of the big populations in this country can make its own plans and contribution to the common stock of knowledge and enter into a glorious competition to make in the progress of years their city more beautiful, more convenient, more commodious, and happier for the human beings who live in it.

In the same way in a city like this, where the intelligence and the moving spirits of industry meet round this table, what an opportunity you have for making your contribution to the solving of the most difficult problem we have to face to-day! There are few here, probably, who believe that the industrial system is static and here for all time. You are all mainly engaged, as I have been, in industry, and have gone through the mill, and we have to move on and realise, as I do, that so far from industry being static it is dynamic. We have to move on into a state of things that has yet to be a better one both for efficiency and in its spirit than anything else that we have yet come through. There will have to be much hard thinking on the part of all who are engaged in industry, whether they be masters or whether they be men; and it will be impossible for the change that I believe to be necessary in the future to come about until there is a very different atmosphere in which to discuss and negotiate those changes than has been the case in the last twenty years.

The atmosphere in those years has been, in many parts of the country, poisoned. I do not wish to say anything here about where the faults may lie. But I do want to say that I realise, as you do, that a great deal of the propaganda which has been done during the last twenty years—the propaganda of a kind that teaches class hatred—has in many places done its evil and its poisonous work.

I am thankful to say that I see signs throughout

the country to-day that those who believe that permanent progress can be made by that method are not an increasing number, but the work that has been done in that direction cannot be undone in a moment. And it will mean the utmost goodwill, the utmost force of example to bring about, to any great extent, something better and something on which we may erect a permanent and stable building. In industrial matters I believe in publicity. I believe, in spite of much that we fear, that the agreement that was made in the mining industry has taught the country a great deal. As you pass away from the days of small businesses into the days of big limited liability companies, your problem is completely altered, and what we have to do—and here nothing can be done without your help—is to humanise the system of limited liability. That is an extraordinarily difficult thing to do, but after all, let us remember publicity. Where there is ignorance there is always suspicion, and until you on your side—I will say we on our side —get the men who work for us to understand our problems, as they do not understand them to-day, you can never hope for progress.

I have often said I regard it of the greatest importance for workmen in industry, and particularly their leaders, to have what some of them already have, a knowledge of the industry that they are in—a knowledge of the finances of that industry, a knowledge of the costs of that industry, a knowledge of the costs of that industry abroad (that they may understand what competition means), a knowledge of the methods of marketing those commodities abroad. It is far more important for them to have that knowledge than to have even the amount of knowledge that may be accumulated after six weeks' sojourn in a foreign country of the language of which they are ignorant.

I am catholic in my views. I would exempt no class to-day from working hard at their own problems. I think those who lead Labour and those who lead the employers have got to work harder at their task of comprehension and of explanation than they have ever worked before.

There is one thing that I have always felt as an employer, and it is this. A good employer is very apt to devote his whole time to his own works, and to refrain from coming out into public life, because he has not time for it, and it perhaps does not attract him, and for some reason he is often reluctant to leave his own place of work. There is one cause in which he should be prepared to sacrifice himself —and it is a sacrifice. I want to see the ranks of employers throw up a man who will lead his men, making it the principal task of his life to be the mediator in all subjects affecting their work, whilst standing up, as he is entitled to do, for the order he represents. There can be no finer career for a young man than to go into business, not with the object only of making a fortune, as he probably would—for any man is worthy of his hire—but with the idea of making his contribution towards getting the whole of these relations on a firmer footing.

There can be no finer work for men who, as boys, went out to France, and learnt what a British regiment was, than to try to get something of the spirit of the British regiment into their industry.

DEMOCRACY AND THE SPIRIT OF SERVICE

From a Speech at the Albert Hall

4th December, 1924

THE responsibility for progress rests not only on the Government, but on every man and woman in the country. The Government can go no faster in progress than the people will allow them to do. Willing co-operation in new methods is essential, and without the will to work progress is not possible, and with constant stoppages of industry progress is not possible. Progress can be obtained by the people of this country if they have the will to obtain it. But just as it can be helped by them, so it can be impeded and retarded and stopped altogether. The ultimate responsibility is with the people more even than with the Government. It is a testing time for democracy. Many are those who would pay, and do pay, lip service to it. But I remember that democracy is after all but the government of the people by the people through their freely elected representatives, and unless the responsibility for that government is felt throughout the length and breadth of the country, from top to bottom, by men and women alike, democracy itself will fail.

Democracy, democratic government, calls for harder work, for higher education, for further vision than any form of government known in this world. It has not lasted long yet in the West, and it is only by those like ourselves who believe in it making it a success that we can hope to see it permanent and yielding those fruits which it ought to yield. The assertion of people's rights has never yet provided that people with bread. The performance of their duties, and that alone, can lead to the successful issue of those experiments in government which we have carried further than any other people in this world. Democracy can rise to great heights ; it can also sink to great depths. It is for us so to conduct ourselves, and so to educate our own people, that we may achieve the heights and avoid the depths.

Closely akin to that comes the subject of our great Empire, on which I would say a word or two. When we speak of Empire, it is in no spirit of flag-wagging. What we feel, I think, is this : we feel that in this great inheritance of ours, separated as it is by the seas, we have yet one home and one people, and we want the realisation of that to be so vivid to our own people that men may ask themselves, as they come to manhood, " Where, in this great inherited estate, can I do best for myself ? Where have I a better opportunity of bringing up my family ? Where can I do best for the Empire ? " When the answer given is " overseas," let us do everything we can to see that the path is made easy for those who desire it, that we may help to spread the peoples of our Empire, the ideals of our Empire, the trade of our Empire from one side of the world to the other. After all, great as the material benefits are, we do not look primarily to them. I think deep down in all our hearts we look to the Empire as the means by which we may hope to see that increase of our race which we believe to be of such inestimable benefit to the world at large ; the spread abroad of people to whom freedom and justice are as the breath of their nostrils, of people distinguished, as we would fain hope and believe, above all things, by an abiding sense of duty. If ever the day should come when an appeal to that sense of duty falls on deaf ears among our own kin, that day indeed would be the end of our country and of our Empire, to which you and I have dedicated our very lives.

And, if I may, a few words in conclusion to you workers from all over the country and to the new members of Parliament who sit behind me. We have to-day perhaps the most magnificent opportunity of service to our country that has ever been given to any party. You who have just been elected to the House of Commons are, by the testimony of your fellow-countrymen, their natural leaders for the next four or five years. It is your duty, your primary duty, to educate that great democracy of which we are all a part. Let me put this to you, to all of us who have passed through the experience of the recent election. Can there be anything that stands before us more clearly or poignantly than the groups of our fellow-countrymen who listened in faith to what we had to say, who trusted us and have given us their confidence, and who believe in their hearts that we have come to London to do what we can to right those things that are hard and difficult for them, and to help them in what is always the difficult struggle that they have in life ? Don't ever lose touch with your constituency ; don't ever mistake the voice of the clubman and the voice of the Pressman in London for the voice of the country. It is the country that has returned you ; it is the country which will judge you.

I was struck two or three days ago by reading the words of an old Oxford economist, with whom I disagree in almost everything else that he ever wrote. He said : " Consider not only the process by which the machinery of our social condition has been made, but much more the opinion and action which has developed and moulded the character of the English people." Do not ever forget the character of the English people, in which character and in love of which character pursue your work and help them.

I want to see the spirit of service to the whole nation the birthright of every member of the Unionist Party—Unionist in the sense that we stand for the union of those two nations of which Disraeli spoke two generations ago ; union among our own people to make one nation of our own people at home which, if secured, nothing else matters in the world. I urge on you all as workers in that great Unionist Party to render all the service you can to the common weal in the districts in which you live. There is always work and to spare for human betterment in every parish in the country. And to all those workers for the Party and members of Parliament, I say this in conclusion : You cannot better serve your Party, and through the Party your country, than in dedicating your lives to that service.

TRUTH AND POLITICS

On Inauguration as Lord Rector of the University of Edinburgh

6th November, 1925

THE first duty of a Lord Rector is to thank his constituents for the honour they have done him in electing him to that great and historic office.

But beyond the honour, of which they are no less conscious than he, lies the unique service unconsciously rendered to a Rector who is normally immersed in public affairs.

Though " to be at sea " is a phrase used by landsmen to denote instability of purpose and absence of sense of direction, it must be acknowledged that we landsmen have much to learn when we are at sea, if we will. We learn that there are two things on a ship that are not done. A sailor does not spit on the deck, thereby strengthening his self-control and saving unnecessary work for someone else ; nor does he speak to the man at the wheel, thereby leaving him to devote his whole mind to his task and increasing the probability of the ship arriving at or near her destination. In matters of State, having selected a man for the wheel, we do everything we can to distract his attention and to prevent him, if possible, from having time in which he may consider for a moment where he is going.

Therein is the service of which I spoke, that you compel your Rector to make time, though it be out of fragments, in which he may reflect on the course of national affairs in a more objective and detached way than is usually possible for him. You force him to pause and ponder and present his reflections for your consideration. It is not surprising if the result is that his thoughts should turn towards you and that he should find himself driven to ask : what is the special contribution which men and women educated at our universities can make to the world ?

You who are students in Edinburgh have a high reputation to maintain. It was of this University that it was once declared by a competent witness :

" I may truly say that it is not easy to conceive a university where industry is more general, where reading is more fashionable, where indolence and ignorance are more disreputable."

I hope you recognise yourselves to-day in the words of Sir James Macintosh, written a hundred years ago.

I shall not pitch my expectations too high. The fraction of life which you spend at the University is small, and there have been other forces continuously at work before you came here moulding your lives. It is the education received unconsciously that counts for most in the making of a man. The

University can only work within the limits of the human material which it receives from the homes and schools of the country. It can provide a favourable soil for the developing intelligence under the supervision of expert gardeners, but it cannot grow figs from thistles.

The University is a rich storehouse of knowledge, and some fragments of its treasures do somehow find their way into the possession of the students. The University is also an instrument for increasing knowledge, and some students, a small proportion, do contrive to add to the accumulated learning of the ages. They settle " ὅτι's business, properly base οὖν, and give us the doctrine of the enclitic δε."

But, besides, or rather in the process of, transmitting and increasing knowledge and training ability, the University is a school of character. That is true not only of the common room and the playing field ; it is also true of the lecture room and laboratory.

The ideal character is a harmony of many virtues, and it is a tradition amongst us to give to truthfulness the position of the cardinal virtue. Hence, for example, the curious power of Lord Althorp, who was known to have said to the House of Commons, " I know this to be right. I cannot remember why —but you may take it that it is so," and they believed him. And if the noblest exercise of freedom is the pursuit of truth, the best equipment for the search is to be truthful. The inculcation of the practice of truthfulness, no less than the acquisition of knowledge, is the motive force of our educational system. The student is here to learn habits of accuracy in measurement, precision in statement, honesty in handling evidence, fairness in presenting a cause—in a word, to be true in word and deed. That is the goal of British education, because it is recognised that no man can be a worthy citizen whose word cannot be trusted and whose deed is compounded of deceit.

Men think by means of words and communicate with each other through their medium. This " most noble and profitable invention of speech is man's proudest triumph over nature, without which there had been amongst men neither commonwealth nor society, nor contract nor peace, no more than amongst lions, bears, and wolves." [1] Words are the currency of love and friendship, of making and marketing, of peace and war. Nations are bound and loosed by them. Three or four simple words can move waves of emotion through the hearts of multitudes like great tides of the sea : " Lest we forget." " Patriotism is not enough."

There is a well-known passage in the writings of John Stuart Mill, where he doubts whether all the inventions of machinery have on balance added to human happiness. I am always reminded by that passage of another in John Locke, where he is so impressed with the defects of language as to affirm

[1] *Leviathan*, I, iv.

that if anyone " shall well consider the errors and obscurity, the mistakes and confusion, that are spread in the world by an ill-use of words, he will find some reason to doubt whether language, as it has been employed, has contributed more to the improvement or hindrance of knowledge among mankind." [1]

The Scottish are cautious, it has been said, because they have lived with one another for so long. You are capable of practising great restraint and economy in the use of words, but I do not think that even you will go as far as Locke and wish to put us all into a Trappist monastery. Such knowledge as there is in the world has been built up by the help of words. A civilisation without words is perhaps conceivable, but under it the life of man would be " solitary, poor, nasty, brutish, and short." But if we cannot go all the way with Locke, we can agree with his successor, Bentham, that " error is never so difficult to be destroyed as when it has its roots in language." " Improper terms are the chains which bind men to unreasonable practices. Every improper term contains the germ of fallacious propositions ; it forms a cloud, which conceals the nature of the thing, and presents a frequently invincible obstacle to the discovery of truth." [2] It is in a similar mood that Mr. Wells complains of the fluidity of thought and the fixity of language. Master

[1] *Essay Concerning Human Understanding*, Book III, Chapter XI, Par. 4.

[2] *On Evidence*, Book III, Chapter I.

of English as he is, he finds its terms solid, opaque, and stable, and therefore "incurably inaccurate." That is not merely a defence of philosophic doubt, but a conclusion of despair which, if we accepted it literally, would close all universities to-morrow and destroy all foundations of belief.

No small part of education lies in learning the right use of words, in tracing their birth and behaviour, in fitting them closely to facts and ideas. That is why you are here invited to study the Humanities not only for their own fair sake, but for the discipline which is experienced in the manipulation of two of the finest instruments ever devised to express the minds of men. Through the Humanities you should learn not only something of the polity and law, the poetry and eloquence of the ancient world, but you should learn the value of the words of your own native tongue. No man who can do good Greek and Latin prose can deceive people with words except he sin against the light. He can no longer be deceived himself. He will know that to use words equivocally is prostitution. Nor does he need to use italics in speech or writing. Headlines cannot hypnotise him, and the latest sensation is already stale.

Through mathematics we learn on the very threshold a lesson which, if universally known and applied, would prevent most of the ills to which the world is heir. To know and realise that two and two make four and can in no circumstances make anything else is to be equipped with knowledge that will save us daily from mistakes, unpleasant to ourselves, and possibly disastrous to others. I know that some of Euclid's axioms, which appear to common sense to be necessary, are now declared by mathematicians " to derive their appearance of necessity from our mere familiarity with actual space, and not from any *a priori* logical foundation. By imagining worlds in which these axioms are false, the mathematicians have used logic to show the possibility of spaces differing from that in which we live." [1] But even these daring speculators assure us that in any possible world they feel that two and two would be four and that this is not a mere fact, but a necessity to which everything actual and possible must conform.[2] Whatever be the case in a world of Einsteins, or in Russia, over most part of the world two and two are still believed to make four. Without that knowledge or in the belief that two and two may in a certain environment make five, you may indeed upset a constitution, but you will never make an engine, nor, if you were in possession of a ship, could you bring it into any port in the world. Those, therefore, who would navigate the ship of State, if they would avoid shipwreck, had better base their sailing orders on this platitudinous verity.

Through all your studies of the physical sciences you are being taught a similar lesson. Principles

[1] Bertrand Russell : *Introduction to Philosophy*, p. 320.
[2] *Ibid.*, p. 121.

are constantly being subjected to the test of fact, purified in the furnace of experiment. Working hypotheses are being confronted with masses of detail, and as a result are discarded, revised, or quickened. You strive to compel the material facts of the world to reveal their nature, you watch and record their behaviour, and truth is the accurate statement of the facts observed. By means of this discipline you learn that things are what they are and the consequences will be what they will be. In other words, that as you sow you will reap, and a wrong combination of elements will send you through the roof when your desire is to remain with your feet firmly planted on the earth.

Lastly, there is the study of the ultimate science, the science of sciences, of moral philosophy for which this University has been so justly famous. There was a time when it might be said that the chief export of Scotland, measured in values, was metaphysics. It was to this University that more than one Prime Minister came from England to sit at the feet of Dugald Stewart. The penetration of English practice by Scottish reflection was one of the most fruitful results of the Union, and is still happily proceeding in the person of our distinguished Chairman (the Earl of Balfour).

Philosophy forces the student to examine the assumptions on which all the other sciences rest, the hypotheses by which they all work. You ask not only How ? but Why ? You challenge all appearance ; you doubt science itself in your search for reality. Magic, myth, ritual, religion ; the mysterious and emotional story of human belief ; the theological speculations of mankind ; the very instrument by which man knows anything at all— all are cross-examined as facts of experience, and an attempt is made to interpret them and fit them into some coherent explanation of our life and destiny. You cannot go any distance on this road without arriving at the distinction between true assertions and false ones, and you will not need to travel much farther before reaching the distinction between right and wrong.

Throughout all these activities in which you are engaged in this University there is the double motive of acquiring knowledge and learning to think truly. The latter is the more important task. The greatest service this or any university can render the modern world is to discharge well this duty which is laid upon it, and to send forth year after year generations of young men and women who have not only a stock of ideas but minds which turn on the poles of truth. Ability to read is not synonymous with ability to reflect on what is read. Better to doubt methodically than to think capriciously. Education that has merely taught people to follow a syllogism without enabling them to detect a fallacy has left them in constant peril. And as with the fallacy so with its near relation, the half truth. For though it has been accepted through the ages that half a loaf is better than no bread, half a truth is not only not better than no truth, it is worse than many lies, and the slave of lies and half truths is ignorance. Ignorance, static and inert, is bad, but ignorance in motion, as Goethe once observed, is the most terrible force in nature, for it may destroy in its passage the accumulated mental and material capital of generations.

You will need this habit of truth when you leave this home of learning and reflection. It is our greatest national asset. The industries and commerce of this country, its enormous foreign trade, involving innumerable transactions with known and unknown customers, has been made possible not only by the enterprise of our merchants, but by their integrity. There is nowhere in the world, I believe, a higher standard of commercial honour than that which prevails in this country. And the same is true of our Courts of Law, which enjoy a world-wide prestige, nowhere better exemplified than in the Admiralty Court, to which shipowners from all over the world resort, even in cases where no British ship is in the collision or salvage operation.

Why is it, then, that when we turn to politics a lower standard of habitual truthfulness is alleged to prevail than in the world of science or of business ? I am not now talking of this country more than another. I think our reputation is at least as good as that of any other country in this regard, and it has grown in the last 100 years, and is growing. The scientist is assumed to be a truth-lover ; honesty is proverbially the best policy in business ; but politicians have been despised for hypocrisy and dishonesty in all the literatures of the Old World and the New. I open the work of a brilliant Cambridge scholar and theologian, and this is what I read on the first page :

" In regard to truth, the more one reads of man's notions about the meaning and method of civil society, the more often is one inclined in despair to say that truth has as little to do with politics as it has with most politicians." [1]

And this is the verdict of a learned foreign observer at the end of an immense treatise on the pathology of party government : " To the low types which the human race has produced from Cain down to Tartuffe, the age of democracy has added a new one —the politician."

What is the explanation of this evil reputation which attaches not to politicians of one party, but to the whole race ? Primarily, I suppose, it is due to the fact that ever since States began to be they have been in peril and have trusted to force for their safety. War has been their normal history. Savagery has never been far away from the realm of law. How long is it since that ceased to be true in Scotland ? With war and the preparation for war go the stratagems of diplomacy, the dropping of the ordinary code of morals, a holiday for truth, and an aftermath

[1] Figgis : *From Gerson to Grotius.*

of cynicism. Force and fraud are in war the two cardinal virtues, wrote the author of *Leviathan*. The statesman's goal is the preservation of the State, and reasons of State have been held to justify all policies whatsoever. In the arena of international rivalry and conflict men have placed patriotism above truthfulness as the indispensable virtue of statesmen. " When the entire safety of a country is at stake, no consideration of what is just or unjust, merciful or cruel, praiseworthy or shameful, must intervene," [1] is a copybook maxim from the pages of a well-known exponent of the art of Government. And it was a statesman much nearer our own time who said to a group of friends : " If we had done for ourselves the things which we are doing for Italy, we should be great rascals." [2] That sounds less shocking to our ears to-day than it would have done a dozen years ago. Machiavelli's conception of mankind has not been dispelled or disproved. He is, as Lord Acton said, a constant and contemporary influence. He is in all our hearts.

We have recently been celebrating the tercentenary of the publication of the work of Grotius on International Law. Dr. Figgis, the Cambridge historian and divine, whom I quoted a moment ago, points out that the fundamental difference between Machiavelli and Grotius is concerned with the question before us. The contention of Grotius, which is

[1] Machiavelli : *Treatise on Livy.*
[2] G. M. Trevelyan : *Garibaldi and the Making of Italy*, Chap. I.

denied by Machiavelli, is that human life is essentially a society, and that certain laws, of which fidelity to plighted word is the most important, are therefore as immutable as human nature. These two thinkers represent two tendencies in our public life. The principles of Machiavelli were accepted in Europe at any rate as late as the days of Cavour and Bismarck. I wish to avoid the twentieth century and examples from among the living. It was the prevailing view for centuries, openly avowed and defended, that you could have one code of morals among nations and another and much more exacting one among individuals, that you could be a Machiavellian abroad and a Christian at home. Whatever may have been our lapses we have never in this country accepted this view in the bald and summary form in which I am putting it. It was, nevertheless, a British Prime Minister who said that " No great country was ever saved by good men," which is perhaps why Lord Acton said that great men were nearly always bad men. But the shifts to which statesmen and diplomatists have resorted in the field of foreign affairs, especially in time of strain or open conflict, have helped to give all politicians a bad name.

The party system is perhaps a contributory cause. The system has its advantages, its team work, its loyalties, and others which I need not stop to describe, especially as the whole subject was most ably analysed by my colleague, Lord Cecil, in his address to the students at Aberdeen a few days ago. To our sporting countrymen it appears a game, and as such it has its rules, and these for the most part are honourably obeyed and are an important help to probity in our public life. But the party system does put a certain embargo on complete frankness of speech in the arena of debate.

But it is to a third explanation that I want to direct your attention for a few minutes more. There is a profound difference in the study of the physical and the human sciences, between the study of particles of matter and of men in society. You cannot measure and weigh, combine and distribute men as you do chemical elements. Spinoza tried something of the sort, but he did not succeed. You remember a famous passage, where he says how he had made it his especial care neither to mock, to bewail, nor to denounce men's actions, but to understand them, how he had tried to consider the emotions and agitations of men's minds, love and hatred, anger and envy, honour and pity, just as a scientist would regard heat and cold, storms and thunder. But though we sometimes speak of rhetoric as hot air, the state is not a cloud, nor, I fear, do we politicians often return in scientific showers the popular vapour which we are said to absorb.[1]

The material of politics is human nature, its motives honourable and base, its appetites for power

[1] *Tractatus Politicus*, quoted in Pollock's life, p. 300 ; cf. Von Hügel, *The German Soul*, p. 67, and Acton, *Historical Essays and Studies*, p. 479.

and for service, its passions, its prejudices, its memories and aspirations. But the politician cannot work with scales and forceps, with test tube and mortar. His instruments are the written and spoken word. Politics can never be an exact science. Democracy is government by discussion, by talk. Politicians must talk, and they cannot to-day, like Pitt, confine their speeches to the House of Commons. The perils of the platform orator have been pointed out from the days of Cleon. Words have lost none of their equivocal character since his day. The difference between the Greek sophist and the modern demagogue, it is said, consists in this : the one displayed his ingenuity by appearing to prove that which his hearers knew to be false, the other displays it by appearing to prove that which his hearers wish to be true.[1] It is the business of the universities to change all this, and they are doing it.

The politician is much nearer in type to the barrister and advocate than to the scientist. The latter has no case to prove, he sits humbly before the facts and lets them speak. The advocate and the politician are more interested in persuasion than in proof. They have a client or a policy to defend. The political audience is not dishonest in itself, nor does it desire or approve dishonesty or misrepresentation in others, but it is an audience only imperfectly prepared to follow a close argument, and the speaker wishes to make a favourable impression, to secure

[1] C. Cornewall Lewis : *Use and Abuse of Political Terms*, p. 12.

support for a policy. It is easy to see how this may lead to the depreciation of the verbal currency and to the circulation of promises which cannot be cashed.

Closely allied with this is the pressure laid upon the politician in a democratic state to speak while important negotiations are in progress, however inconvenient the moment. The result once more is inevitably to place a veto on complete frankness, and to tempt recourse to words which are nebulous, hesitating, ambiguous, or misleading. Some of us have become as adept as the Prague poet who went to see Béranger in 1847, and had to answer a few questions. Was Prague in Hungary or in Poland? In neither one nor the other. Was Bohemia in Austria or in Germany? In both. Was the Prussian monarchy absolute or conditional? Partly one, partly the other. At last Béranger lost patience : " Frenchmen," he cried, " like things to be clear. What is not clear is not French." [1] If the subject is one of high foreign policy the wrong words may raise issues not settled by dropping pieces of paper in a ballot box but by dropping bombs on cities. That is the essential difference between the methods of politics and of business.

In these directions we may discover some mitigation of the harsh epithets used of the politician.

I come back to where I began. False words, said the dying Socrates, are not only evil in themselves,

[1] Acton : *Historical Essays and Studies*, p. 474.

but they infect the soul with evil. Although the use
of words may be abused and the fight for their
honour may at times seem hopeless, we must never
give up the struggle to use them solely in the service
of truth. Let us aim at meaning what we say, and
saying what we mean. The price man has to pay
for the good things he enjoys is constant watchfulness
lest they be employed for evil. Has not this been
the case from the dawn of history with drink,
language, and liberty ? Let us—in the language of
Leviathan—use perspicuous words, having first
snuffed and purged them from ambiguity and made
them luminous. Let us take our stand on public
right and a law of nations with Grotius rather than
with Machiavelli ; let us seek to moralise our public
intercourse and reduce the area of casuistry and
duplicity. That is not only the accepted principle
of the best amongst us, but it is, I am sure, in harmony with a widespread instinct in the British
people. It asserted itself in August 1914 when it
was made plain that ethics was not a branch of
politics, but the reverse. It is at the root of our
support of the League of Nations at Geneva—a city
with which Scotland has had spiritual ties for
centuries, and from which your Churches derive
their system of regulated freedom. It is truth alone
that will " destroy the face of the covering cast over
all people and the veil that is spread over all nations "
(Isaiah xxv. 7). There is much that is profoundly
wrong and remediable in our civilisation, but let us

not lightly discard the gains so hardly won from the savagery which so readily besets us. In stretching forth our hands to the farther shore, let us realise that civilisation itself is but the ice formed in process of ages on the turbulent stream of unbridled human passions, and while this ice seemed to our fathers secure and permanent, it has rotted and cracked during the agony of the Great War, and in places the submerged torrent has broken through, leaving fragments in constant collision threatening by their attrition to diminish and ultimately disappear. The more need for you, the lampbearers of your generation, to guide your own steps by the truth, and to light the way for the wandering people of the world.

RHETORIC

AT THE CAMBRIDGE UNION
March, 1924

I SOMETIMES think that possibly a man's views of rhetoric may be coloured according to whether he possesses it or is without it ; this may be the reason why Mr. Mitchell Banks, who has made such an eloquent plea, finds himself in opposition to me. I have never been a rhetorician or an orator. I attribute this largely to the fact that, much as I used to enjoy reading speeches, I was greatly struck when I was about eighteen, at coming across a phrase in Froude, " Oratory is the harlot of the arts," illustrated, as Froude could illustrate it, with a wealth of eloquence ! There is nothing odd about that, because you will remember that there was no one who fulminated more against rhetoric than Carlyle, probably the greatest rhetorician who ever put pen to paper. I was reading in him only the other day that the best thing man could do was to doom himself to eternal silence, which Carlyle never could do, except when he was smoking a pipe with Tennyson.

Mr. Theobald (the mover of the resolution) made

a most characteristic remark in his definition of rhetoric, a definition on which a good deal depends. He defined it as a marshalling of facts which were likely to persuade people. I entirely agree with him, except that he has left out the other half of the sentence, which is the essence of my case : " Concealing the facts which are likely to dissuade people." There is a good deal more in rhetoric than the marshalling of facts, otherwise the *Origin of Species* would have been the greatest work of rhetoric the world has produced.

To tell the truth needs no art at all, and that is why I always believe in it. We have each attempted our own definition of rhetoric. I would rather define it by illustrations of what I mean by rhetoric, which I regard as one of the greatest dangers of modern civilization. I am going to give you two or three phrases which I call rhetorical phrases, and each of them, to my mind, is pregnant with darkness and confusion. Consider this one of three words from one of the greatest rhetoricians of the ages : " Bulging corn bins." " The democratic control of the means of production " is another. I tried in the House of Commons to get that last phrase translated from rhetorical English into English that I could understand, and the only answer I got was that it was impossible to produce rabbits from a top hat. " Self-determination " is another rhetorical term that may some day lead the nations into a bloody war. That is what rhetoric does. " Homes fit for heroes to live in," and " A world safe for democracy ! " These, to my mind, are the quintessence of rhetoric, and it is against rhetoric in this sense that I am going to vote to-night.

I suppose every one will admit that a great rhetorician was Charles Fox, who said something which illustrates my point very clearly : " If a speech reads well it must be a damned bad speech." I mean by this that Mr. Mitchell Banks will read his speech to-morrow morning with less pleasure than that with which he heard the cheers for it to-night. Rhetoric is meant to get the vote of a division or at an election, but God help the man who tries to think on it !

Such speeches as have been quoted in support of rhetoric could not be delivered nowadays. The character and temper of the audience and the people have so changed that what may have been possible for Macaulay is impossible to-day. The rhetoric of to-day, the rhetoric we have to consider, is the rhetoric of the " Bulging corn bins." I suppose that this gift has been responsible for more bloodshed on this earth than all the guns and explosives that have ever been invented. If we look back only over the last century, was there anything more responsible for the French Revolution than the literary rhetoric of Rousseau, fanned by the verbal rhetoric of Robespierre and others, just as the Russian Revolution was due to the rhetoric of Kerensky—flatulent rhetoric which filled the bellies of his people with the east wind ?

That appalling twopenny-ha'penny gift of fluency, with the addition of a certain amount of training and of imagination in word-spinning, is the kind of rhetoric which stirs the emotions of the ignorant mob and sets it moving. It is because such forces can be set in motion by rhetoric that I have no regard for it, but a positive horror. Very rarely do we find the gift given to men who have wisdom and constructive power, and for the time being it would seem that it was in this world a force far beyond its merits, although in the more advanced countries I sometimes hope that it is past its prime. At least I believe that in England and Scotland at any rate rhetoric of the kind I have tried to describe no longer makes that appeal to the people.

I think it may be that the people of this country are getting just the least bit suspicious of the literary rhetoric of our Sunday Press, and of our daily Press, and that this very wholesome dread, this wholesome nervousness, is being transferred from the Press to the platform. I think that throughout this country there is to-day a far greater desire than there has ever been before to hear plain, unadorned statements of cases. I believe that anyone who has taken part in recent elections—a few constituencies excepted—will agree with me that one of the most remarkable features is the way in which large audiences all over the country will listen to a statement of a case, whether they agree with it or not, provided they feel that the statement is made honestly and fairly, and with due consideration for the opposite view.

Let us always remember this : when we come to big things we do not need rhetoric. Truth, we have always been told, is naked. She requires very little clothing. After all, St. Paul was no orator, and yet his speeches and his teaching seem to have spread and to have lasted a long time. I cannot help feeling that if we were to go back two thousand years I would back St. Paul and the results of his teaching against all the rhetoric of a Sunday paper or of the leading orators of the age.

If there is one thing which those who have been in any other profession than the Bar distrust more than another it is the eloquent man. In the business world, other things being equal, the man who has the power of talking is not the man who gets promotion. To be able to express oneself in business is always to be written down as being not quite first-class, and it is a joyous fact that in most of the towns of the kingdom we find that the men of business who talk most in such places as Chambers of Commerce are not the men who are making a success of the big businesses in the country. From this I argue that it is not necessarily the man most fluent of speech to whom we should entrust the destinies of the country.

ON LITERATURE AND THE ARTS

THE CLASSICS

To the Classical Association
8th January, 1926

THE Classical Association flings its boundaries far and wide, embracing as it does the learned and the simple, the just and the unjust, the half-timers, the whole-timers and the over-timers, the leisured, the wealthy and the poor. All that is asked of a prospective member is that he should love the Classics. Love does not necessarily imply comprehension, or which of us could say that he loved a woman ?— but it does mean love of the beautiful, love of the best, love of the ideal. Such love is not rare, and it is well that those who have it should join together and gather strength and refreshment by such communion as the present. I can speak of these things with understanding, for I am an original member of the Association, and I well remember the pleasure with which I sent my first subscription from the depths of the country in which I was then living and received in due course the annual volume of the *Proceedings*, together with the President's Address for the year. It seems to me now, as it seemed to me then, that there could be no greater honour than to be invited to give the Presidential Address. It never occurred to me that that honour was to be mine. I certainly had no qualifications for it, nor indeed have I now. But I take heart from the thought that though the lamp of classical learning must be trimmed and kept burning by the scholars, yet the light which is diffused depends to some extent on the fuel, and that is provided by an army of plain folk with conviction and enthusiasm in their hearts.

The Classics will never perish out of the land so long as they are cherished by ordinary people. And so it seems to me good that you should have a President occasionally who is not a scholar, who is not particularly distinguished, but who can speak for the common folk as an ordinary man.

I wonder how many of you remember your Eginhard ? I have always had in mind a passage of his which I read forty years ago. Charlemagne was a statesman, but not a scholar. He acquired such knowledge of Latin that he used to repeat his prayers in that language as well as in his own. Greek he could understand better than he could pronounce. But he was an ardent admirer of the liberal arts, and greatly revered their professors, whom he promoted to high honours. He also tried to write, and used to keep his tablets and writing-book under the pillow of his couch that when he had leisure he might practise his hand in forming letters ; but he made little progress in a task too long deferred and begun too late in life. *Absit omen!* And since I have alluded to the weakness of so great a man in his pronunciation of Greek, perhaps I may take advantage of this opportunity to seek on my own behalf your indulgence if, in the few Latin words that I may use hereafter, I pronounce Latin as it was taught to me fifty years ago. I have lived for many years in a backwater, and the flood of culture has swept forward far away from me. I speak not as the man in the street even, but as a man in a field-path, a much simpler person steeped in tradition and impervious to new ideas. To pronounce Latin as our Association has decreed may be to Professor Postgate the breaking of an adhesion ; to me it is to convert it at once into a foreign language. And I have been the more impressed that my experience is not void of truth because I noticed with interest, when my own University did me the high honour of conferring a doctor's degree upon me, each learned man who had occasion to speak the Latin tongue spoke it with a different accent. Is my apology accepted ?

Before I attempt to tell you what I conceive to be the debt of the ordinary man to the Classics, may I, as one whose work has for many years past been given in the field of politics, pause a few moments to inquire what help our studies may bring to the ordinary man who is attempting the task of government ?

To be an Englishman, native of a country which was an integral part of the Roman Empire for a period as long as from the Reformation until this present night, and to be ignorant of the history of that Empire, is to be without that sense of perspective in viewing both the change of events and their day-to-day reactions which is essential to see our national life and to see it whole.

Ne sutor supra crepidam may be true for the cobbler, but the statesman must endeavour, like the sculptor, to envisage the whole figure, and he must be steeped to the lips in the historical sense. It was not for nothing that Western Europe was forged on the anvil of Rome, and who can say how much we owe to those long years of Roman law, Roman discipline, Roman faith, and partnership in a common Empire ?

During the first four centuries of the present era Roman thought and Roman manners imposed themselves upon our island and made themselves a home here. Rome must have seemed very real and present to the children of the near-by hamlets as they saw the great roads creeping towards them, past them, and ever onwards in ruthless and undeviating course, making the farthest ends of the island pervious to the legions' tread. Shy traffickers coming from wild fastnesses as they chanced upon a Roman highway and, shading their eyes with their hands, saw it pass into the horizon, must have been awed at the thought of the great heart that beat at the end of that giant artery. Beautiful buildings, kindly plants and flowers now so familiar came in the wake of the eagles and sank their foundations and their roots in English soil. It may well be that sub-conscious memories of those days and the mingling of blood for four centuries played their part no less than the arrival of the Normans in modifying certain characteristics of our Teutonic invaders and saved us from becoming what Carlyle called " A glutton-ous race of Jutes and Angles, capable of no grand combinations, lumbering about in pot-bellied equa-nimity ; not dreaming of heroic toil, and silence and endurance, such as leads to the higher places of this universe and the golden mountain-tops where dwell the Spirits of the Dawn."

Only a few short centuries before the age of Pericles, only a few short centuries after the fall of Troy, there was but a settlement of shepherds on the Palatine Hill. Yet within a thousand years the tramp of the Roman sentinel was heard along the Wall ; his watch-fires illuminated the waters of Euphrates ; the hand of Rome reached from the Biscay to the Euxine, from the Danube to the Nile.

Here is the greatest, most fascinating problem in all history for the scholar and the statesman. Why did the Empire come into existence at all, and why, having come into existence, did it perish ? Volumes have been written on the subject and will continue to appear; but is it not allowed to the statesman whose material is human nature to dwell on one aspect of the story to the exclusion of others, equally obvious and equally true? Surely the character of the Roman played as great a part in the rise of the Empire as his character played in the fall? I can imagine no historian of the British Empire neglecting the study of the character of the Englishman, as shown, for example, in the Elizabethan age and through the period of the Rebellion. And to me the outstanding and peculiar strength of the Roman character lies in the words *pietas* and *gravitas*. These were the foundations of a patriotism which alone could carry the burden of Empire, a patriotism innate, a motive force of incalculable power, yet something at its best so holy that it was never paraded, sought no reward, was taken for granted, and had no single word to express it.

Bounded at first by the confines of the city, it differed from Greek patriotism in that it had in it the seeds of life and growth, and it expanded with the spread of the Roman name. Such patriotism is not unknown amongst us, and so long as it exists it will leaven much. As has been well pointed out, the highest gifts devoted to public service were expected; to dedicate and employ them for the sake of the Republic was merely your duty. Aristides would not have been called the Just in Rome, and in what country in the Ancient World but Rome would a Fabricius have refused all rewards, or a

Cincinnatus have returned to his farm ? Again, a character founded on *pietas* and *gravitas* had its roots in truth, and I am proud to think that the English word has been held in no less honour than the Roman. It would be an interesting study to trace the changes in the Roman character which accompanied the social developments through the chequered history of the Empire. This is the happy task of the historian, and it must suffice for me in these few minutes to pause before certain salient facts. It is from Ammian, who wrote while the legions were leaving Britain, that we learn that the Roman word could no longer be trusted. That is to me a far more significant portent than the aggregation of the population in cities, the immense luxury, and the exhaustion of the permanent sources of wealth, all of which combined to sap that very character whose continued existence was necessary for the life of the State. We hear through these later centuries cries with which we are only too familiar to-day, cries against the burden of armaments and the weight of taxation. But above and beyond these things, dangerous and symptomatic as they are, we detect a greater cause for anxiety. It would almost appear that the human stock is like the stock of fruit-trees where the best kinds tend to work themselves out after many generations of useful and productive service. Mr. Mackail, in one of his recent Essays, has laid fresh stress on this point when he says there were not enough Romans left to carry on the work of Rome. A gradual atrophy of intellectual energy and public spirit spread over the body politic, and the instinct of self-government was lost. There are fears amongst those who are responsible for government to-day, fears not yet gripping us by the throat but taking grisly shape in the twilight, that the Great War, by the destruction of our best lives in such numbers, has not left enough of the breed to carry on the work of Empire. Our task is hard enough, but it will be accomplished; yet who in Europe does not know that one more war in the West, and the civilisation of the ages will fall with as great a shock as that of Rome? She has left danger-signals along the road; it is for us to read them.

And as we do so we may look, as she did, at another history. That Roman Empire, of which we were once a part, embraced all the countries occupied by people of Hellenic blood. Less in the direct historical succession, though more in the spiritual, the statesman has much to learn from Greece. Her history, as has often been pointed out, is one long failure to create an Empire. Her problem was nearer ours in kind than that of Rome, for her solution, had it been effected, would have resulted in a Commonwealth of Nations rather than an Empire on the Roman model. There was no experiment she did not try to win organic unity, but she was defeated by those very characteristics of intellect and temperament which raised her to such heights in poetry, art, and philosophy. Civic unity she could never achieve, and her attempts to weld together people of the blood were foiled on the very threshold. Failure is in many ways a more potent teacher than success, and the tragedy of her history only throws into more radiant relief the debt we owe her in those arts wherein she was supreme. She spoke the last word in beauty of speech and of form ; her creations are the touchstone to-day as they were two thousand years ago, and it is a comforting thought, in these days particularly, that whatever fails to pass this test must ultimately perish from among us as barbarous and exotic.

And here, perhaps, we may take two thoughts to heart which come to my mind as I try to look forward. Believing as I do that much of the civilisation and culture of the world is bound up with the life of Western Europe, it is good for us to remember that we Western Europeans have been in historical times members together of a great Empire, and that we share in common, though in differing degrees, language, law, and tradition. That there should be wars between nations who learned their first lessons in citizenship from the same mother seems to me fratricidal insanity. It should rather be our endeavour to help ourselves and to help each other to recover those qualities of character so peculiar to the Romans, the *pietas*, the *gravitas*, and the truth of the spoken word. On such foundations alone can civilisation be built ; on such foundations alone can civilisation stand.

But what of us, the *ultimi Britanni*, the youngest member of the great family ? I like to feel that the fortune of the youngest son is ours. I like to picture the procession of the nations through the ages as a great relay race of heroes. Over a course infinitely hard, with little experience to guide her, Rome ran her mighty race bearing her torch on high. Of those who came before, of those who followed after, none ran so far, none so surely. And when her course was run the torch came into other hands who bore it forward according to the strength and guidance that was in them, until after many centuries it was passed to us, the youngest son. Our race is not yet run. But we shall run more worthily so long as we base our lives on the stern virtues of the Roman character and take to ourselves the warnings that Rome left for our guidance.

Here I feel these modest reflections may well be brought to an end. I can imagine you saying, " Well, there may be an element of truth in what you have said, but it is all rather jejune and second-hand. What we want to know is, the impression the small amount of Latin and Greek which you possess has made upon you ; what you think you have derived from it, whether you are in any way richer than you would have been had you been nursed on the Loves of the Triangles." A perfectly fair question, and I will bid the statesman fly away and the ordinary man step forward.

Most of those whose real application to the

Classics came to an end with their school-days will recall their early studies as being in so large a measure a struggle to acquire the form that the matter at the time impressed itself only secondarily on the mind. The strange words betrayed an obstinate angularity ; no inflection was so minute that it could be disregarded without prejudice to sense ; even their place in the puzzle was significant ; and if in use they were roughly treated or jumbled together without due order, they refused either to reflect things or to express ideas. But imperceptibly this very quality disciplined the mind to realise that the words had a definite value. When rightly used, moreover, it seemed that these unworn words would give forth our thoughts or express a meaning with a directness and immediacy lacking even in our own speech. Perhaps it is that many centuries have elapsed since those words had been bandied about in everyday speech, and hence they have a freshness and keenness of impression which no vulgar association has had the chance to blur. In our own time the words which build up the most exquisite poem, we have known to be used in other contexts—to have provided a rhyme for a sentimental song or patter for a low comedian. It may be that when the trireme's rating in the Piræus found his rations short, or the centurion was jostled in the crowded byways of the Suburra, winged words used by Homer or Virgil were pressed into the service of each to become the vehicle of their complaint and abuse, and that these same words in their day had many a frivolous or debasing task to do. But none of this has reached our ears ; all the multitude of tongues which echoed in the Agora and Forum are hushed in silence and oblivion ; and to listeners across the centuries alone of all the sounds of ancient Greece and Rome " still are their pleasant voices, their nightingales awake." Ruskin once said, " All inferior poetry is an injury to the good, inasmuch as it takes away the freshness of rhymes, blunders upon and gives a wretched commonality to good thoughts ; and in general adds to the weight of human weariness in a most woeful and culpable manner." But the literary works of Greece and Rome which have reached us come burdened with no such poor relations ; the poets whose reciting in the month of August was such a plague to Juvenal and his contemporaries have not survived to weary us, and everything second-rate has long fallen by the way into the gap of centuries over which only an eternal merit has enabled the survivors to waft themselves. Due again to the freshness of the words is another feature of the ancients' writing, its clarity and its conciseness. It cannot fail to strike the merest beginner who tries to translate our tongue into Greek or Latin, or *vice versa*, in how much fewer words in the old languages the thought can be expressed. It is distressing to find ourselves saying in ten lines what the Roman said in five ; but at least it may give rise in us to a conscious effort to tighten up the belt of our speech, when we see the sentences of the ancients clean run like athletes and fit for their work as compared with the prolapsed and slovenly figures of so much of our own diction. Moreover, the ancients did not over-elaborate their thought, being content to leave something to the mental processes of their readers. How different from so many of our English scribblers who seem to have taken to heart Wilde's dictum that "nothing succeeds like excess," and who swathe the thinnest of thoughts in a profusion of words in the hope, maybe, that it will appear larger from its wrappings. Even our great writers are sometimes too eager that nothing that can be said on the theme they take shall remain unsaid, or any germ remain undeveloped to which the reader's own mind might give increase ; and they are apt so to run their thought to a stand-still that no potentiality remains in it to set the reader's mind agog. Why do we all know about the beauty of Argive Helen ? Not because Homer gave us a catalogue of her charms with exhaustive precision, but just because he gave a hint and left it to us. I think he says no more than that, as one day she passed upon the walls, the elders said it was no wonder that for such loveliness men should die and cities should be sacked. Her loveliness is left to each of us to envisage as we will, and thus it is that it lives afresh in a myriad forms, newborn throughout the centuries in each man's heart.

The form then is ever fresh, and I have spoken of

it first because to many of us so barely initiated this has made the earliest and most immediate impression. It is perhaps only as we get older that the beauty of the matter unfolds itself and reveals its eternal significance against our day-to-day experience.

The literature in which peoples with such an outlook found entertainment and instruction was not composed of novels or problem plays dealing with heroes and heroines struggling in the little traps that their own weakness had sprung for them, or with situations brought about by mean mistakes or obliquities of character. What was portrayed in the tragedies of the Greeks was nothing less than the human spirit at grips with the toils of destiny itself. As Seneca said, "A strong man matched with fortune is a sight for the gods to witness." For their characters and situations they had their beautiful mythology to draw on, and the materials which this provided eclipsed altogether the themes which ordinary everyday life could suggest. Always in these tragedies we are secure in the confidence that the characters will not prove unequal to the doom they have to bear ; as it becomes more instant and inexorable so their spirit becomes more indomitable to meet it, and it is never otherwise than the mighty who is " mightily laid low." Whether it is a demigod like Prometheus or a man like Œdipus who is on the rack ; whether their sacrifice to what they deem their duty is demanded of a wife like Alcestis, or a young girl like Antigone, they show us one and all the spirit which is unperturbed by trial and un-diverted by catastrophe. It may be said that this high bearing in trials so profound or so remote avails little to guide us among our practical daily perplexities ; but surely the Greek tragedy, though not drawing on the smaller issues of life for its themes, shows how these should be faced by por-traying to us the serene and the right spirit towards the ultimate issues.

If I may now strike a personal note, I think what I have gained is some sense of proportion, a standard of values, and a profound respect for the truth of words, which have been of use to me in my daily life. Add to these the perennial happiness I am fortunate enough to find in the sheer beauty of Latin and Greek and the thousand images they call up in the mind, and I am indebted to my early training more than I can ever hope to repay. I remember well the first election I fought. It was what was called an old-fashioned election in an ancient borough now disfranchised. The candidate was expected to spend three evenings a week during the time of his probation in one or another of the public houses which jostled each other through the constituency, listening to and vociferously applaud-ing what, for want of a better name, was called, on the *lucus a non lucendo* principle, comic or humorous song. After a time I felt the need of a moral purge and a literal sedative. It was the work of a moment to find what my soul needed. When I came home at night from these orgies I seldom went to bed without reading something of the *Odyssey*, the *Æneid*, or the *Odes* of Horace. By the date of the election I had read all the last-named, and most of the others, not without labour in the dictionaries, not always with ease, but with care and increasing joy; and with the desired result that, though defeated, I had passed through the fire and the smell of burning was not on my garments.

Two years later, by my admission to the House of Commons at a by-election, I entered formally on political life. The possession of a sense of proportion, of a standard of values, and of respect for the truth of words proved an inestimable aid to political judgment. So far as I have had a sense of proportion it has helped me to assess the personal equation of the individuals, distinguished and un-distinguished, who form the House of Commons. So far as I have acquired a standard of values, it has helped me to estimate speech and the written word, and has saved me many a time from bowing to the idols of the market-place. So far as I have had respect for the truth of words, I have been helped to detect the fallacy and the equivocal phrase lurking in the tropical growth of oratory, and I have endeavoured to use a speech plain and unambiguous. I have also been able to enjoy with unmixed pleasure the choice of words and the phrasing of those speakers who model themselves on the classical tradition. Without a rival in that style I would place one of the most distinguished members of this Association, the Earl of Oxford. Amongst our great speakers we have those whose inspiration is obviously of Athens and those whose debt is to Rome. The Earl of Oxford is a Roman in his lucidity, in his phrasing, in his felicity. It requires but little stretch of imagination to picture him in the Courts delivering a defence, shall we say, *Pro Georgio*, or in its greatest day addressing the Senate in a speech which for its incisive and dexterous advocacy, its compact and pregnant sentences, would be the despair alike of the translator and the most experienced writer of Latin prose.

And let me add in a sentence, a political leader should know his *Knights* by heart, for there is no profounder truth than that the sausage-seller lies ever on the flank of Cleon.

But over and above these qualities which delight the intellect, there is the more subtle, deeper something which touches the heart and soul. The voices that speak to us across the death and rebirth of nations touch every emotion of each succeeding generation in these later days, as they touched those who had ears to hear in Athens and in Rome ; but they reach us with the added solemnity and pathos which cling to remembered sayings of those we have loved and lost. Every ultimate problem was theirs, as it is ours, and the more you open your soul to their appeal the more profound your pity for stumbling humanity, the more eager your effort to bind together

the family of man rather than to loosen it.   It is
no blind chance that has led one of our greatest
scholars to devote his life to the ideal of the League
of Nations.   Rather it is his desire to make his
contribution to redeeming the failure of those very
Greeks whom he, more perhaps than any living man,
has helped this modern world to understand.

But we are linked together in the shallows no less
than in the deeps.   Need I quote *Diffugere nives* to
those whose first home was in the country ?   Is not
everything in those lines ?—the passing of winter
and the feathering out of the trees, the assurance of
every spring in every world that ever was ?   How
many a holiday and home-coming are recalled by
the words,

peregrino
Labore fessi venimus larem ad nostrum
Desideratoque acquiescimus lecto.

Have we not the eternal youth of the world in *dulce
ridentem* and *gratus puellæ risus ab angulo* ?—a score
of words and we see our own childhood, our children's, and every generation from the beginning to
the end of time.   What memories such lines call
up !   They knock at the heart like the drum taps of
the Fifth Symphony.

I have little more to add.   If I have convinced you
of my sincerity as a member of the Association, I am
happy.   I may repeat to you what I have said to my
friends, that when my work in politics is completed
I shall take down all my old companions from my

shelves and work once more with dictionary and grammar. I have always kept the embers aglow that they may easily be blown into flame to warm my senile bones.

I cannot end without an allusion to the Anthology which my dear friend Mackail has done much to make known to English readers. I would remind you of the epitaph on the Athenians who fell at Plataea : the lines might have been written for our own youth which hastened out to Flanders that late summer, eleven years ago :

Εἰ τὸ καλῶς θνήσκειν ἀρετῆς μέρος ἐστὶ μέγιστον
ἡμῖν ἐκ πάντων τοῦτ᾿ ἀπένειμε Τύχη·
Ἑλλάδι γὰρ σπεύδοντες ἐλευθερίην περιθεῖναι
κείμεθ᾿ ἀγηράντῳ χρώμενοι εὐλογίῃ.

We stand together with bowed heads in a sorrow and pride that reach across the centuries.

I remember many years ago standing on the terrace of a beautiful villa near Florence. It was a September evening, and the valley below was transfigured in the long horizontal rays of the declining sun. And then I heard a bell, such a bell as never was on land or sea, a bell whose every vibration found an echo in my innermost heart. I said to my hostess, " That is the most beautiful bell I have ever heard." " Yes," she replied, " it is an English bell." And so it was. For generations its sound had gone out over English fields, giving the hours of work and prayer to English folk from the tower of an English abbey, and then came the Reformation, and some wise Italian bought the bell whose work at home was done and sent it to the Valley of the Arno, where after four centuries it stirred the heart of a wandering Englishman and made him sick for home.

Thus the chance word of a Latin inscription, a line in the anthology, a phrase of Horace, or a " chorus ending of Euripides " plucks at the heart-strings and stirs a thousand memories, memories subconscious and ancestral.

SHAKESPEARE

AT THE CITY OF LONDON SCHOOL
13th June, 1924

I VIVIDLY remember a Prime Minister, no less a man than Mr. Gladstone, coming down to my school Politically opposed to him as I was, I waited eagerly for the message. Just before Mr. Gladstone's visit I had had a difference of opinion with my Headmaster, and relations were somewhat strained. When Mr. Gladstone opened with the words " Your admirable Headmaster," I felt that the Prime Minister was so out of touch with the whole of the life I was leading that I never listened to another word.

You who are here are entering into a blessed heritage that is the peculiar right of our own people. I am proud to be on the platform with Sir Sidney Lee, against whose shield all the iconoclasts of the world break their spears. Some wish to tear the laurels from Shakespeare's brow to place them on the brow of Bacon ; others say that *Wuthering Heights* was not written by Emily Brontë : and some even say that Mr. Lloyd George did not offer ninepence for fourpence. Long may their spears be broken !

I understand that Shakespeare is a compulsory subject at the School : do not rush to the conclusion that a man is any the worse for being a compulsory subject. When I was a boy I knew the *Odes* of Horace backwards and forwards, and when I came to manhood year by year those odes came knocking at the door of my heart at the most unexpected times and places. So, even if you do not realise it now, the time will come when you will be thankful that you were steeped in Shakespeare as boys. In him we not only have, as Sir Gerald Du Maurier said here not long ago, perhaps the greatest man the world has ever seen, but one who had a profound knowledge of human nature and of the world. Shakespeare was one of those few poets in whom we find the magic which comes straight from heaven, and which is the prerogative of the very greatest : such magic as we find in the poetry of Keats, in the first scene of the last act of *The Merchant of Venice*, and throughout the sonnets.

Shakespeare's plays, no matter of what country he may be writing, are redolent of our own soil and of our own country people. The habit of thought and the outlook of Shakespeare's country people and of those wise men, Shakespeare's fools, may be found to-day in our rural counties. It is no mere coincidence that the School's " Beaufoy Day " was originally 23rd April, for besides being Shakespeare's birthday, it was St. George's Day. That brings us back to England.

The City of London is famed for so many things that people sometimes fail to realise what she has done for the education of our country people. Your School is the last of the great foundations for sending trained men into the world that is left within the boundaries of the city. One by one they have gone—Christ's Hospital, the Charterhouse, the Merchant Taylors'. I hope the City of London School will always remain as a witness to the great light that has burned throughout the ages in this great city.

You have a tremendous responsibility on your shoulders. Not all the tradition, not all the great men who have gone before, can keep our country as she should be kept, unless in each generation are found the men who will take the torch from the generation that is passing, keep it bright and hand it on.

To-day there are many things we have to struggle against in England, but the greatest is the loss of the men from the ages of twenty-six or twenty-seven to forty, the flower of the nation's early manhood that lies in France and Belgium. Not only have we lost the benefit of the work they might be doing to-day, but the natural leaders of the young men coming along are the school generations immediately preceding them, and the generations coming to manhood now are deprived of that natural leadership of the elder brothers who were at school about a decade before. The burden and the responsibility falls heavier, therefore, on those who have just come to manhood and on those about to do so. Never has the need of the country and of the world for men trained as you are being trained, been so great When you come out into the larger world, though you may find the struggle harder than it has ever been, yet there is a warm welcome awaiting you from those who to-day are bearing the burden and the heat. You will find, too, a world that has never been more in need of the service that can be given by men with trained minds and clean, sound bodies.

BYRON

It is very difficult during a man's lifetime, or in the years immediately succeeding his death, to make any just estimate of his fame. The Reverend John Todd, who wrote a *Students' Guide* shortly after Byron's death, told his students to beware of bad books, and included Byron's works and Walter Scott's together. As was his duty, he had read those books, and was convinced that Byron's works would quickly pass from notice and be exiled from the shelves of virtuous men. That is a contribution of literary taste and puritanism from the United States.

About the same year a young critic wrote of the peculiar strength evolved by Byron, a man who gave the world a better heart and a new pulse. That was Alfred Tennyson, who at the age of twenty-five put his finger on one of the causes why Byron's Centenary is being celebrated to-day.

What magic is it that brings people together a hundred years after the death of a famous man ? The man who finds new pulses in the world is the man who will enjoy immortality. Byron was, if anything, a sower of new seed that had a great germinal force. It is difficult to realise what that force was when it first appeared, unless we can put ourselves in the place of the men who read his first poems. At the time the first cantos of *Childe Harold* appeared the Continent for nearly a generation had been a sealed book to travellers, owing to the European wars; the Mediterranean, now known to almost everyone in England, was practically an unknown sea; and too often those who had escaped abroad went with no eyes to see. Byron found the eyes of the people sealed, and opened them, and for that reason the gratitude of the nation should be given to him. The spirit at home and in Europe was waiting for such a revelation as Byron had for it. In the epoch which immediately followed he pushed the Romantic movement begun by Scott with a strength and power which Scott himself could not achieve, and no one was quicker to recognise the genius of the younger man than that great-hearted poet himself. The spirit existing both at home and in Europe at, and after, the end of the Napoleonic War was the spirit that was waiting, all unconsciously, for the revelation that Byron had for it. It wanted, perhaps, without knowing it, force, strength and movement, and those things Byron gave as they had never been given before.

These things alone might not have made his name to-day what it was in his lifetime, but there was added the personality of which his contemporaries told, the loss of which made Scott say, " It is as if the sun had gone out."

The side of Byron which impresses me most is that of the great and persistent workman in his high profession of literature. He worked as an artist must work if he is to leave his mark on coming generations. That is the part of his life which he kept to himself as the holiest and best to him, and he knew, as great artists do, the worth of his own work.

Beyond all men Byron was happy in his death. I could not help thinking as I walked to this commemoration what a different history it might have been, what a different celebration might have been held in after years, if Byron had lived to return from Missolonghi. But in his death he established his immortality, and words not to be lightly used of any man might be used of him :

" If to die nobly be the chief part of excellence, to us of all men fortune gave this lot, for, hastening to set a crown of freedom upon Hellas, we lie possessed of praise that grows not old."

It is praise, which grows not old, for a man who grows not old, that is his immortality, and it is that immortality we are here to salute.

W. H. HUDSON

AT THE UNVEILING OF THE HUDSON MEMORIAL IN HYDE PARK

19*th May*, 1925

WE are gathered together this May morning to honour a rare and remarkable spirit. It is more than eighty years ago that Hudson was born in a land where, to use his own words, he heard " the little yellow finches in thousands amid the millions of pink peach blossoms, pouring out wonderful music against the blue sky." Yet just as those who grow older feel increasingly the pull of that earth from whence they are sprung—and to none is that pull stronger than to those who have had the joy to be raised in the red earth of England—so he felt the pull of that soil of Devonshire whence his forefathers had come.

Fifty years ago he landed in England, unknown, unheralded, unadvertised, and the greater part of those years were years of infinite struggle and toil. There is one thing which is not generally known, and which is a tribute rare in itself and significant of that high sense of honour and pride which was his. Early in the century the Civil List did honour to itself by giving him one of those small pensions which are within its competence. Then, a few years ago, when his wife died and his meagre income was minutely supplemented, he surrendered that pension at his own desire and in spite of the protests of those administering it, because he felt he could do without it and that, infinitesimal as the relief would be, he did not wish to let another grain of sand add to the weight of the already overburdened taxpayers of the country.

It has been a frequent experience in our history for Englishmen and Scotsmen to go out into the wilds of the earth and to come back and tell us what strange things they have seen ; but Hudson came from the ends of the earth and rediscovered to the people, many of whom even if they had eyes saw not, and if they had ears heard not, something of the beauty of their own country. He it was who made familiar to thousands the hidden beauties of our southern counties. He taught Londoners who had never heard of them the names of places like Whitesheet Hill, Chilmark, Swallowcliffe and Fonthill Bishop—names of beauty and romance which always fill me with profound gratitude that the names of flowers, of villages, of stars and birds, were given in those dark centuries, long before our people were educated and had the advantage of cheap literature and a popular Press.

There were a few things which raised passion in Hudson : one certainly was the felling of the big elms in Kensington Gardens and the destruction of the Rookery ; another was the sight of people whose palates could only be tickled by larks' or plovers' eggs ; and another was the sight of ladies who had ransacked the hidden corners of the earth to decorate their hats. I think that to-day we are doing national penance for the sins we have committed in the past, and are resolving so far as we can to abstain from offence in the future.

It is not for me to say anything of Hudson as a writer, but I would like to remind you of Joseph Conrad's remark : " One can't tell how this fellow gets his effects ; he writes as the grass grows." We cannot tell how anyone in the finest literature gets his effects, but we thank God for the effect.

There was one thing which bored Hudson, and that was politics, but it is only fair to remember the impartiality of Hudson's admiration for politicians. There were only two he could tolerate : one was a Liberal, Lord Grey, and the other a Tory, Lord Banbury. He was attached to them for obvious reasons: to Lord Grey for his love of nature and to Lord Banbury for his hatred of cruelty to living creatures.

In making this sanctuary a memorial to Hudson, we are doing something that would have touched his heart. The world never needed sanctuaries more than it does to-day. In old days it was compara- tively easy for a man to run away and hide himself for a time in the desert or the monastery, but the spread of civilization has rendered that impossible.

Mr. Cunninghame-Graham has spoken of St. Francis feeding the birds, but to-day St. Francis would be snapshotted, birds and all, to form an exclusive picture the next morning. There are three classes which need sanctuary more than others : birds, wild flowers and Prime Ministers. Prime Ministers want some place where they will not be snapshotted, where they can be private, and where they can perch for a moment on a fence and look at the landscape without being " shooed " off. Thanks to Lord Lee, I have my sanctuary at Chequers, and therefore I feel it incumbent upon me to be here to-day to open this sanctuary for my fellow-sufferers who find London at times a little crowded and a little lacking in that privacy they require for their best development.

There is another reason why we are beginning to feel the necessity for something of this kind. Those of us who love the country and country things feel in our bones the urbanisation of our land and the need that something should be done to preserve our birds and our flowers. It behoves us all to act because of that love which exists in English people wherever they may be found, the love and craving for beauty which they can rarely see, rarely know, and rarely realise in their own lives. We ought to do everything we can to foster that spirit, and it is in the belief that this day we are helping to draw people's attention to bird life that I rejoice to be allowed to unveil this memorial.

ART

Dinner of the Artists' General Benevolent Institution

6th May, 1925

On an occasion such as this I recall my boyhood days, when some of my excitements consisted in coming to London from Worcestershire to visit my uncle, Sir Edward Poynter, who then lived in Wood Lane. It was a little old-fashioned country house with a garden, where now there is the power-station of an electric light company, and opposite, where the White City stands, were open fields. The friendship which I enjoyed with my uncle was one which lasted from the earliest days I can remember to the day of his death. I made my first acquaintance with Italy as a young man in his company.

It is strange and curious to look back on those days, and to remember that atmosphere of art and culture, of wit and humour, and to recognise what one owes to it. One learns, in having the privilege in youth of mixing with men like that, and their friends, the inestimable value of such an association for after life, even for one who has taken a far

different career, and who, owing to a strange con-
catenation of circumstances, finds himself to-day
Prime Minister. I learnt there, all unconsciously,
the value of work. The men I am thinking of were
workmen, first and foremost. They were men who
worked at what they loved and who felt that it was
due to the art they loved to give it every power that
God had given them. If, at any time, they went for
holidays they painted all the time, because they liked
it. That is the secret of good work, and the secret,
incidentally, of happiness. They would never
tolerate scamped work. Burne-Jones, a keener
critic of himself than any of his outside critics were,
knew perfectly well where his own defects lay, and
he worked for years in middle life to master that
draughtsmanship that he had not learnt as a young
man, because his decision to become an artist was
only taken after he had left Oxford. All men who
love their craft, and who believe in it and live for it,
are their own best critics. I learnt from this man,
in addition to the value of work, a complete indifference to all criticism, except that which combines
the two essential gifts of sincerity and truth. I also
learnt from the quality of those men and their friends,
and from the conversations I unconsciously heard,
to form my own standards of value in after life,
rather than to attribute brilliancy, as I am so often
asked to do in London, to something that I know is
in itself essentially second-rate. I say these things
to explain why I am present on this occasion. I

know that if any relations of mine, to whom I have referred, had happened to die before they had achieved fame and reputation, their widows and orphans would have been dependent upon the funds of this institution (the Artists' General Benevolent Institution) for their livelihood. Therefore, I feel that I owe it to the memory of those I loved, who have played so large a part in my own spiritual and mental development, to help in however small a degree by saying something in aid of this great charity.

Art, in popular estimation, is going up in the world and politicians are going down ; but the time was, and not so long ago, when if a man died who had been an artist, unless he had the good fortune to be a baronet and a millionaire, the newspapers always said, " The deceased, much against his family's wishes, became an artist." At that time it was thought a very desirable thing to be a statesman. I am not sure that to-day in the obituary notices you may not read that the deceased, much against his family's wishes, had embraced politics as a career.

I would like to emphasise the absolute necessity of the artist giving his whole time to concentration on his work, just as in political life a man has to devote his whole mind and strength to the almost superhuman task which is imposed upon him, and to confine his attention strictly to his work, lest the quality of that work should suffer.

The present are difficult times for those who try to live by the profession of art of any kind. They are difficult because times are bad. There is not a great deal of money about in this country, and we are not a people who naturally spend money on the encouragement of art if we can spend it on anything else. Those who have the most money, millionaires, not unnaturally are in the hands of the dealers.

One of the great difficulties always seems to me, as an outsider knowing nothing of these matters, to be that there has been worked up an entirely fictitious value in the pictures of the dead. I hope this may arise from a high motive ; from a feeling that having let many artists and poets in the past starve in their lifetime, we should allow them to provide a living for anyone who can make it out of them. When a very rich man wants to invest money in pictures, he wants to invest it in something that will not lose its value, and as long as the dealer keeps up the value of the old masters he knows it is safe. But if he wants to buy a modern work of art he has to exercise his own judgment, and if his judgment is wrong he loses his money. So the artist to-day, however good he may be, has everything militating against him. There may be prizes from a worldly point of view for the few, but in these days there must be, financially, only too many failures ; though whether they fail or succeed they have a real pleasure in the actual performance of their work. Taking artists as a whole, whether they have been what the world calls successful, or not, they are a very happy confraternity. The artist and the poet can, and often do, solace themselves with the thought that if the people of this generation do not appreciate their work, they may yet be painting or writing for generations to come, and the thought of recognition by posterity, provided that the wolf is kept from the door, is in itself a great comfort and strength.

ARTISTS AND POLITICIANS

AT THE ANNUAL BANQUET OF THE ROYAL ACADEMY

2nd May, 1925

I SHOULD like, if I may, on behalf of my colleagues who are here to-night, to congratulate you, Mr. President, on your election to the great office which you hold, and to express our sympathy with the Academy in the loss they have sustained in the death of Mr. John Sargent—a great man, as well as a great artist. His memory will be cherished through his paintings, and his art will be a prized possession of posterity. And, Sir, I should like to congratulate you on this singular achievement in getting together an assembly of such distinction in London on a Saturday night. I remember trying to secure an eminent Englishman as a much-desired trustee of the National Gallery. He was a master of English and a scholar, and so he was able to express himself as I could not when he declined that great honour. He wrote to me : " No ; they have a damnable habit of holding their meetings on a Saturday."

Now I understand these are friendly gatherings

at which confidences may be given and exchanged, and I should like to tell you something of the difficulties of a Prime Minister's life. A Prime Minister has to form a Cabinet. I reflected when I was making mine that I should have to appear to-night at Burlington House, and I thought the greatest compliment I could pay the Academy would be to include, if possible, a painter in the Cabinet. I thought I would choose someone who could paint with a broad brush, and I regret extremely that he, at the last moment, had to cancel his engagement here to-night. I need hardly say I refer to the Chancellor of the Exchequer. When I had secured my artist, the question was where to put him. I at once decided that the right place for him was where he would have problems to study of currency and exchange, and where he would be dealing with mathematics. Many of my critics were hostile, but they were not astonished. If they had known their Plato they would have known at once why I asked him to go to the Exchequer. Many here will remember what Plato said to the Delians. When the oracle set a problem, Plato said : " It must be supposed not that the god specially wished this problem solved, but that he would have the Greeks desist from war and wickedness and cultivate the Muses, so that, their passions being assuaged by philosophy and mathematics, they might live in innocent and mutually helpful intercourse with one another." It is an extraordinary thing how the solution of many of our difficulties was really found many years ago.

Now I said there were many points of resemblance between your careers and ours. Neither artists nor politicians can by any figure of speech be said to belong to organised labour. Labour, yes; organised, no. What power have we to strike? If every artist in this country laid down his brush to-night, would a ripple pass over the country? If I laid down my brush to-night, are there not fifty men who would be ready to take it up? But then, on the other hand, you cannot be nationalised, and neither can we. It is sometimes to your advantage, and sometimes the advantage rests with us. Now take criticism. We both either suffer or enjoy criticism. There I think the advantage is with us. We, if we think fit, can answer back. These canvases on the wall have to take it in contemptuous silence. Your instruments by which you work so well are dumb—pencils and paints. Ours are neither dumb nor inert. I often think that we rather resemble Alice in Wonderland, who tried to play croquet with a flamingo instead of a mallet.

Then, again, with both of us, to achieve success it is necessary to mix our colours, so as to produce a harmonious whole. But your colours have an advantage over those which are mixed on our palette. In the language of the trade, your colours are fast; ours are not so necessarily. You mix your colours to form a harmonious result, but it may be after four or five years some of the colours, which you thought the most beautiful, have faded and have been unable to stand the bright light of day, and those which you thought mixed well in the general scheme have come up hard and crude and dominate the whole picture. We politicians are, and must of necessity be, impressionists—impressionists, because we want to catch the public eye, and we hope that we can make our meaning clear. We also trust—my colleagues and I—that people will not examine our workmanship too closely, lest they find defects in it which are not visible at a distance. But there is one thing in which you have a great advantage. If when you complete a piece of work you do not like it, you can put your boot through it. With us the boot is on the other leg.

I have noticed sometimes that advice is given to the artists of this country to make a clean sweep of the Academy. It is always a revolutionary people who think a clean sweep must result in something which will give keen satisfaction. While, in the last four years, the Academy has remained without great change, we have made a clean sweep of three Governments, and we have a fourth in—and yet people are not satisfied. So may there not be something said even for keeping an Academy or keeping a Government ?

There is one thing that we do have in common. No man in politics can ever hope to achieve his desire

—he can never accomplish the veriest fragment of what he would will to do. In the same way, in the breast of every artist who is an artist—and it is not everyone who uses a brush who is an artist—there is a secret known only to himself and spoken of to none—that ideal which he is ever seeking and ever following up, and never in this world captures. It is that which drives men on to their best and finest work. I doubt if any real artist has ever satisfied himself. Occasionally, there comes what Kipling has called the " magic," whether it be in poetry, in prose, or in art, before which the voice of criticism is dumb—the art that speaks straight to the soul of the world. Few of us can hope to achieve that, and I think perhaps if I were to choose any words with which to conclude, I would choose those that may be taken either for your work or for ours—the words that Browning put into the mouth of Andrea del Sarto :

> I, painting from myself and to myself,
> Know what I do, am unmoved by men's blame
> Or their praise either.

ON EDUCATION

SELF-EDUCATION

AT BIRKBECK COLLEGE

20th March, 1924

THE faith that can remove mountains was the faith of the pioneers of Birkbeck College, and some of them lived to see the College as we know it to-day—a solid, stable and permanent institution. It is a great and triumphant story of which you may well be proud. But I think that it would be useful to remember that if you wished to understand history and sympathise with the founder and pioneers of the College, you must not make the fatal mistake of reading our history to-day, or of a hundred years ago, in the light of the present time ; you must try to throw yourselves back a century, and consider a few of the ways in which the training you have had may help you in your after life.

A hundred years ago popular education, so far as any one thought of it, was regarded as a dangerous explosive. Those times have passed. A hundred years ago London was a comparatively small city

compared with the one we know. There were no
police. The parish constables were not allowed to
go beyond the confines of their own parishes, and
the night watchman kept the peace of the city. Old
London Bridge was still in existence. Waterloo
Bridge had only just been built. Gas had only just
been introduced into the streets when the first
students came to the College. Contrast the position
of the Press to-day with what it was in those days.
At that time there was a bye-law under which no
man who contributed to the Press was eligible to be
called to the Bar, and the Lord Chancellor of the
day caused great consternation and indignation
amongst his friends by asking the editor of the
Times to dine with him. To-day, which of us
would not feel proud if we were asked to dine with
a newspaper proprietor ?

Again, to touch upon another aspect of life, the
Elizabethan Poor Law was still the law of the land.
Of the million and a quarter people in London at
that time one in every eight was in receipt of Poor
Law relief.

But hardly ever in the history of our country, or
of any other country, was there a more wonderful
and brilliant period in the literature of England than
in and around the years when the College was
founded. It shows that, although in many ways
the country was what the people of to-day would call
backward and unprogressive, yet a literary movement was going on which would be a glory to any

country for all time. I need only name Sir Walter Scott, Wordsworth, Byron (who died in 1824, within two years of Keats and Shelley), Carlyle, Tennyson, John Henry Newman (one of the greatest masters of English prose), Thackeray, Browning and Dickens. There was a galaxy of talent of the highest order in a literature that stands second to none in the world, and it was a great thing that the College took its origin from such a time. No country can compare with our own in the literature of that period, and yet at that time there was Goethe in Germany, while Dumas had just gone to Paris and was to present in the succeeding year his first play. That amazing efflorescence in literature was accompanied, as sometimes it is, by an efflorescence in art and music.

I have always firmly held that there is no race with more ability latent than our own, or with a higher aptitude for mechanical genius. When the College was founded, Hargreaves, Arkwright and Crompton, all sons of working men, were inventing the machines which brought in the cotton industry. I mention these names to show the stuff of which our people are made, and how that stuff is worth training and educating. It would be a very interesting subject, for anyone who cared to explore it, to see how many of the mechanical inventions which are light-heartedly attributed to Americans are really the product of British brains, whether they were British brains which have gone to work in that country, or the brains of children of British parents who have gone there. But, having regard to the foundation of this College and the men who went to it in its early days, it is a wonderful thing to reflect that practically the Industrial Revolution, for good or evil, was the work very largely of six or seven men who sprang from the ranks of the people, with no advantages such as you have had ; and that they were men who changed the face of the country and the habits of the lives of the people.

It is probably true that the great number of men who sacrificed their time and their leisure to work and study did so to help themselves to get on in life. But that was not the fundamental reason : there lay behind it the desire of knowledge for its own sake, the will to force a way through those doors that lead to a kingdom of beauty, literature and art.

I am a fair sample myself of the evening student. Many people tried to educate me, but the reaction was not always successful. A great part of my education took place after I had gone into business, on railway journeys and at odd moments, and for some years, when I was working all day, I would read nearly every night. This was the education, I feel, that did me most good. I learned that all of us have to work hard for our living. Some may do work they enjoy ; some may not. Then there comes a time when one feels that one is no use, and that the work itself is difficult and sordid. It is at these times that we may thank God for what we have learned in any school which will enable us to get away from our surroundings into an inner secret chamber. From this we may go with renewed strength to any work that is toward.

There are many definitions of education. The first thing is to be master of our own job ; but to be educated we must know enough of the other man's job to be able to understand the part he is playing in life, and to play our own part in sympathy with him. We have also to learn to play our part as members of the commonwealth, or, in other words, to have humanity, by which I mean the knowledge of the things that pertain to humanity, of the way to go about among our fellows, ready to help and to sympathise with them. Do not go through life as a perpetual blister.

If it be not heresy to say so, do not pay too much attention to examinations. Do not be afflicted with pride of intellect. In my view, pride of intellect is more vulgar that the pride of the *nouveau riche* in his wealth, for the simple reason that the *nouveau riche* has made his own money, whereas your intellect is the gift of God. You may polish it up and get the best out of it, but for the instrument you are less responsible than any man.

Just as I would advise no man to become a political leader—although political leaders are neces-sary—so I would strongly advise no man to become merely a specialist. Always have other interests which will keep you in touch with your fellow-men and women. There is no real republicanism except that of literature. If I find a human face light up at some quotation which everyone ought to know, that man, be he duke or dustman, is my brother. That is the bond of literature. Study it, the glorious literature of the first country in the world—your own.

POLITICAL EDUCATION

AT THE PHILIP STOTT COLLEGE
27th September, 1923

AMIDST all the multifarious duties that fall to my lot, some pleasant and some less pleasant, you have combined to give me to-day a really happy afternoon's outing. I have the greatest admiration, Sir Philip, for this great work upon which you have embarked. It is the grain of mustard seed which will become a great tree that may overshadow the earth, and I am proud to meet so many of those who are fired with the same enthusiasm that you have and that I have for education of the kind that you provide here. It is a great privilege to be allowed to speak to you for a few minutes on that subject. There are few movements in this country in my view that augur better for the future, or that in themselves bear a higher and truer tribute to the best that is in our nature than the great, voluntary efforts that are being made in this country for adult education ; and if there be anyone here who may at times feel a passing regret for the closing of the great houses of England, it must be an immense consolation to see from the ashes of the past springing up a new and hopeful life like this within their walls. That can do nothing but good for the men who come here, and for the country of which they are a part.

I have a peculiar sympathy with adult education, because I have followed it to the best of my ability all my life. I was very much interested to find a peculiar instance recently of that interest which all English people take in education, not always instructed, but always present, because, when I became Prime Minister, a well-known lady in society whose acquaintance I had not had the pleasure of making, asked this question of a friend of mine : " Is the new Prime Minister what you would call an educated man ? " I doubt very much whether she knew what was implied by the word " educated " ; but it showed, at any rate, that she felt that education was a good thing in itself, and a thing which it was desirable should be possessed by anyone aspiring to the post of Prime Minister. That is all to the good. But I expect all of you have learned, as I have, that education is a process and a thing that is never finished. And it is a wonderful thing that here, in this movement, we find one more instance in our history of that triumph of voluntary effort from which have sprung all the best movements and the best things in our country from the beginning of its history. You take a movement like that of the Boy Scouts ; it did not originate with the War Office. You take the Salvation Army ; it did not come from

Canterbury. The Franciscans did not come from Rome ; and in the same way this great movement of education did not take its origin in Whitehall. It sprang—where all these things have sprung from—it sprang from the very heart of the people, and that is what gives it its strength, and that is what is going to continue to give power to the movement.

I was very impressed by a few words that I read in a prospectus of the College, that the aim of the curriculum here is " to furnish instruction which will equip the trade unionist or the co-operator, on the one hand, to take an active and effective interest in the affairs of his or her society, and on the other, a Parliamentarian or a business man to discharge with greater knowledge and insight such duties of citizenship as may devolve upon him."

These words go right down to the root of the matter, because the great task of this generation, in my view, is to save democracy, to preserve it and to inspire it. The ideal of democracy is a very fine one, but no ideals can run of themselves, and if democracy is to be preserved and yield the fruits that those who believe in it would fain see, the only way it can be done is by all the individuals, according to their power, equipping themselves sufficiently to keep the whole mass sweet and true, and to preserve in their plenitude and sanity the ideals that inspire them. I have used this figure of speech before, but I want to use it again. All government of the people can be represented, as it were, on the circumference of a wheel, and government runs in very varying degree from the most complete and absolute autocracy, step by step, to chaos, and you find instances in history of governments passing through every phase on that circumference ; often autocracy will end in chaos, and chaos will, with equal infallibility, lead back once again to autocracy. Now we are at a point in that wheel, and that point is Democracy, with representative government. We have to remember that the price of liberty is eternal vigilance, and, I may add, eternal knowledge, eternal sympathy, and eternal understanding ; and it is our duty in this generation to keep the State steady at the point to which we have attained, knowing full well the risks that lie on either hand by slipping back in the one direction of the wheel or the other, the one direction drawing to a curtailment of our liberty, the other direction being that in which liberty tends to licence.

Now, surely, when we want to educate ourselves for the purpose of citizenship, whatever the immediate course of study may be, whether it be history or economics, whether it be humane letters, whether it be mathematics, the object of such education must always be the same, and to my mind the purpose of such education—a purpose which we try to put in our mind—is always twofold ; it is, in the first place, to clear the mind of cant, and in the second place not to rest content with having learnt enough to follow the syllogism, knowing perfectly well that to follow the syllogism alone is a short cut to the bottomless pit, unless you are able to detect the fallacies that lie by the wayside. If you can clear the mind of cant and detect the fallacy, whatever guise it may be wearing, I think you have made a long step forward in the education that every citizen in a democracy that may hope to endure must have. I think that we all of us realise to-day that no civilised community is bound necessarily and by an inscrutable fate to progress, that there are such things in civilisation as checks, that there is such a thing as retrogression, and that the mere existence of a civilised community is no guarantee either for its continuance or for its progress—in other words, that unless we are the faithful guardians of such civilisation as we have already attained to, we run the risk of seeing the whole of the progress that has been made with such infinite labour up to our own time gradually slipping back and back and back.

No one had harder words to say than Lord Morley about teaching carried on in any other spirit than that which I have endeavoured to describe. Teaching, above all things in this world, ought to be absolutely honest and absolutely free. The teacher should never be the servant of the State in this way, that he preaches and teaches what he thinks the Government would like to have him do, whether that Government come from the Right or from the Left or from the Centre. The whole object of the teacher should be to set forth the truth as he conceives it, and the whole object of the pupil should be so to prepare and develop his mind that he may, as occasion arises, when he leaves here, find himself prepared by will and competent by training to exercise a right judgment in all things.

Lord Morley, when he had laid stress on the everlasting importance of sifting the value of evidence and recognising how the bias of human nature so often prevented men from acquiring the necessary ability so to sift evidence, referred to those who taught with bias and for propaganda in this way : " There are limits to our patience with the quackish fungoids," and it is the " quackish fungoids," wherever they may be found, that you have to go out into the world to fight. " Quackish fungoids " are found in all sections of the community and in all schools of thought. They are not inherent in any one class. They are not necessarily inherent in any one party ; but they are growths which must be cleared away if progress is to be made in our country, and they are growths which the training you receive here will enable you to do your part in clearing away when you leave these pleasant surroundings for the stress and the struggle of the larger world outside.

We have to learn—and it is no easy lesson—to submit all the passions and prejudices which the best of us find to be component parts of ourselves at times to the stern and acid test of the discipline of truth. That is not an easy lesson to learn, or more people would have learned it ; but I think one of the most hopeful signs of the times to-day is that all over the kingdom—north and south and east and west—there are men and women who, in dreaming of a better and higher future for their country, are yet well aware that that future cannot be attained by dreams alone, and they want so to qualify and equip themselves that in that struggle for better things they may be able to play a potent and a worthy part. There is no better and there is no higher ambition, and I am perfectly certain that it is to help that ambition that Sir Philip Stott was moved to do what he has done, a great work for which every one in this room is indeed grateful, a work for which, if I am right, generations yet unborn may arise and call him blessed.

This country of ours has been the birthplace and the home of some of the greatest movements that have yet arisen for human freedom and human progress, and the strength of our race is not yet exhausted. We have confused ourselves in Great Britain of recent years by a curious diffidence, and by a fear of relying upon ourselves. The result has been that many of those who have been eager for the progress of our country have only succeeded in befogging themselves and their fellow-countrymen, by filling their bellies with the east wind of German Socialism and Russian Communism and French Syndicalism. Rather should they have looked deep into the hearts of their own people, relying on that common sense and political sense that has never failed our race, from which sufficient sustenance could be drawn to bring this country once more through all her troubles. There will be found that sense which, far from following at the tail of exploded Continental theorists, is ready once more to lead the way of the world as she was destined to do from the beginning of time, and to show other peoples, many peoples who have not yet learned what real political freedom is, that the mother of political freedom is still capable of guiding the way to her children and her children's children.

Do not let us ever be confused by the advance in material prosperity and material knowledge, and let us never confuse mere acceleration with civilisation. Civilisation is a far deeper and more profound thing than that, and there is a very real danger, in an age when science makes such wonderful advances and can bring so much in the way of material comfort and material knowledge before people without any trouble on their part to acquire it or understand—there is at that time a very great danger that the higher, the more spiritual, the only lasting qualities of civilisation may be submerged in the lower and inferior, so that the last state of that community may be worse than the first.

Then, I think, there is one other great advantage to be derived from the whole-hearted pursuit of knowledge, which has been the impelling force that has brought you from all over the United Kingdom to take advantage of the course which you can obtain here. I think you learn—not by being taught, but by that instinct which comes with wider knowledge —you learn a healthy distrust of rhetoric. If there is any class to be regarded with suspicion in a democracy it is the rhetorician—the man who plays on half-educated people with fallacies which they are incapable of detecting. More than one democracy has been wrecked by that. We do not want to see a democracy like ours, in which we have faith, and which we believe is destined to do such great things for the world, wrecked on any such ignoble rocks. When I was about eighteen years of age, I remember reading a verse of Froude's, in his *Short Studies*, which made a profound impression upon me at that age, because, when I was a boy, as is the case with many other boys, I was rather the slave of fine language and beautiful expression, and I suddenly came with a shock on the words : " Oratory is the harlot of the arts." There is profound truth in that, and I should like very much, if I had time, to give the members that as a text for an essay. It would be very interesting to see the illustrations which historical students might give in proof of the words of that thesis.

There are few things, again, to which, at the present day, we should pay more attention than this —and this again needs education, and the education which you are giving yourselves to enable you to accomplish the end in view—and that is to judge of the value of evidence. I suppose there is no man to whom the cause of the education of the people in this country—and very largely adult education—is nearer the heart than it was to a great Englishman who has just died, I mean Lord Morley. Lord Morley spoke on this subject nearly fifty years ago, and he came back to it again and again ; so recently as just before the war, speaking to the Manchester students, he used these words, which I feel I must read to you :

" Generous aspiration, exalted enthusiasm, is made to do duty for renewed scrutiny. The ardent spirits see every fact or circumstance that makes their way and are blind to every other. Inflexible preconceptions holding the helm, they exaggerate. Their sense of proportion is bad."

There can be no greater object of true education than to teach and to preserve a sense of proportion, and it seems to me that the great advantage you have here over what I may call the definitely propagandist schools is that you have every opportunity of learning to exercise a trained sense of proportion, because the teachers here are chosen in exactly the same way as the teachers are chosen in the free and open universities. They are chosen because they are masters of their subjects. They are chosen not to give propaganda ; they are chosen to speak the truth, and those who are responsible for the conduct of this college know that it is only by giving students the opportunity of exercising to the full the ability that is in them that they will be able to choose the truth honestly and freely, and will exercise their minds to the solution of the problems to which they have to devote themselves, without bias and without preconceived notions. They will clear their minds of cant, and try to see things as they are.

We all of us want understanding—understanding of ourselves and understanding of our brothers and sisters—and that true understanding is the salt that savours the whole life of the community. It was never more needed than it is to-day, and those who understand will realise that there is no greater need in the world, abroad and at home, than peace, peace from the warfare of arms and peace of spirit. Those are the things I intend to fight for during the time that I am Prime Minister, whether that time be long or short, and it is with that object—the object of peace above and before all things—that I am endeavouring to-day to deal with the situation in Europe.

This is not the place to talk about foreign politics. The Imperial Conference meets next week, and it must be that at one of their early meetings the whole question of the present situation in Europe and in the world must be set forth and debated. I would only say here these few words. When this Government came into office, now some ten or eleven months ago, there was an atmosphere of restraint, almost of distrust, between France and ourselves ; and I have no doubt that if Mr. Bonar Law had been spared to us as Prime Minister a little longer, he, with his knowledge, with his instinct, with his transparent honesty, would have dissipated that atmosphere once and for all. But he left us before that task was accomplished, and it was my good fortune in an interview which I had last week with the President of the Council in Paris to help, as I believe, to restore that atmosphere of confidence which had for some time been lost. No more and no less. But I think there is now, both in Paris and in London, a recognition of the importance of the Entente—in this way, that without it a European settlement is far more difficult. Indeed, the events of the last two or three weeks have proved that, to those who have eyes to see, the best hope of settlement lies in intimate relationship between France and this country, and if anything occurred that might keep our two countries apart, then I fear it would make the problems which we have to face incomparably more difficult than they are to-day.

You have been extraordinarily kind to me in the reception you have given me here, a reception which touched my heart, and I just want to tell you before I sit down what a close sympathy I have with you in the work you are doing here. I am a sort of half-educated fellow myself. I worked fairly well at school. I did nothing at the University. I have been trying hard ever since to try to catch it up. You have come here to try to catch it up. I wish you all success and happiness in that task. There is no joy in this world like learning. The great joy of life is that it is a task which is never done. Go on learning all your life. I am learning now, and I mean to go on learning if I live to be a hundred. There is nothing I look forward to so much when I am out of office as to start learning again in real earnest. Until that day comes I am afraid I shall have to leave the learning to you, but I do wish you the best of luck in this high task you have undertaken. Do not let yourselves be dispirited when you get into the world again, but hold fast to what you believe to be true and what you believe to be right wherever it leads you, and whatever difficulties you may encounter. Whatever troubles you may have you will, at all events, always have the comfort of a conscience which will tell you that you have tried to act up to the highest lights that are in you, and you will feel that you are playing your part in helping to bring your country, your fellow-men and women, through one of the most difficult times that she has ever had to face in her history, and that you are laying, or trying to lay, the foundations of a happier, healthier and saner life for those with us now and for those who will come after us.

TEACHERS AND TAUGHT

AT THE ANNUAL DINNER OF THE LONDON TEACHERS' ASSOCIATION

28th November, 1924

GREAT as your necessities may be, mine are greater. I was invited to be your guest when I was but a private individual, before I became Prime Minister. I would add that forty years ago all the king's horses and all the king's men would have failed to have drawn me into the presence of a company of schoolmasters, and in relation to them I once had every qualification as a passive resister and a practiser of very skilled "ca' canny." But times have altered, and I with them, and I am proud to be your guest to-day, to stand before you, not as an educational expert, nor—God forbid !—as an intellectual, but merely to convey to this representative body of London teachers my own appreciation as head of the Government and that of my colleagues of the work that the whole body of teachers throughout the country are doing for the people of this country. Nor do I propose to do what is so common, and to take a gloomy and pessimistic view of the state of our country and of education. I am not going to tell you that in foreign countries they do these things better, and I would observe in passing that we have had some respite recently from that continuous praise of German systems of education to which we were so accustomed in our younger days, and which ceased with such startling suddenness ten years ago.

The progress of education in our own country has, indeed, been remarkable, having regard to the fact that we have only occupied ourselves seriously with the problem for two generations. I know as well as you that there are still too many, far too many, insanitary schools, and that there are many ill-nourished and defective children ; but let us remember that the standard by which we judge these matters to-day has risen immeasurably from the standard adopted by our parents.

You have only to read Sir George Newman's reports of recent years to see the progress that has been made, and, while we can still point to short-comings, to apathy and negligence on the part of parents here, local authorities there, and possibly even sometimes of a Government or a teacher, yet we have to remember that the average health of the children is, and has been, steadily improving, and you have a steadily diminishing quantity in the number and the danger of the children's ailments. Thanks to the co-operation with you of the medical and nursing agencies, of the devoted services of many voluntary agencies, and thanks, too, to the increasing co-operation between teachers and parents, there has never been so much organised effort in this country on behalf of child welfare as there is to-day. We do not ignore the blemishes and the spots, but let me remind you again that we regard them through a far higher magnifying lens than we used to; but that need not prevent us from advancing all the time. I am credibly informed that the children to-day actually enjoy going to school. That is a revolution for which no historian or sociologist has given you adequate recognition. I do it to-night, but I confess that if I am correctly informed you have succeeded in working a miracle which would have been incredible in my younger days.

I agree with Mr. Samuel in this, that no one who lived through the Great War, and was in a position to observe what was taking place, will ever forget the qualities displayed by the men and women of this country, men and women who had had no other education than the elementary schools had afforded them. There are some words of Mr. H. G. Wells which are well worth remembering in this connection. He says that education is one of the newest of the arts and sciences. The idea of particular exceptional people pursuing learning has been familiar to the whole world for scores of centuries, but the idea of preparing the minds of whole classes or communities for co-operation and common action by a training in common ideas is a comparatively new one. And that is the gigantic task to which you, and, I may add, we, are all committed. We are living in days in which the powers that used to be inherent in birth and privilege are passing rapidly away. You have a franchise vested in millions where it used to be vested in thousands, and we live in an age when the preservation of such civilisation as we have already succeeded in attaining to can only be maintained by the spread and continuance of education of the people. And it has never been more urgent to wage the war of reason against the passion that may be stimulated by mob psychology.

Scientific men—and I am afraid I must confess I am not a scientific man—are rather pessimistic, and one of our leading biologists has recently declared that the more representative Parliament becomes, the more unintelligent, as things are, it is and will be. That was, as a matter of fact, written before the election. But I never allow myself to be depressed by the utterances of theorists, and I mean to go on, in conjunction with Lord Eustace, Mr. Samuel, and all of you, to try to make things better. You have handicaps to fight against, handicaps of the bad environment where your children are raised, handicaps of heredity. We can do something to help you, and we intend to do it.

But I always think that those who speak of us who try to direct affairs of State, and of you, use the wrong analogy when they speak of us as builders and architects. Our task is more homely, and, if I may go to the country for my illustration, our work is more the work of the gardener. We have to do our utmost to secure for the child what the gardener does for his plants—the best soil and the best exposure. We must remove the noxious weeds, we must do root pruning, we must prepare and enrich the soil. But we have to wait in faith for what comes later, and that is the flowers and the fruit, and we must remember that we can never hope to gather grapes from thistles. I said the Government might do something to help. I said in the Albert Hall some months ago that I wished to see secondary and university education brought within reach of all children who were fitted to take advantage of them, and I stand by that.

I hope that before we reach the middle of this century the country will have dealt effectively with the problem of the children between the ages of twelve and eighteen. It is not simply a school problem; it is a school problem and an industrial problem. We must by voluntary agencies and by our own work deal with that problem, or we run the risk of allowing a generation to grow up in the country which can only be a peril to itself, and a peril to the nation.

But all the State can do will be of little avail if you have no regard to the one thing that matters,—as always, the personal equation. That, in this case, is the general body of the teachers who are both in love with their work and properly equipped for it. It is for that reason that I welcome the improvement in the pay of the whole profession which came into force in this country of recent years. The personality of the teacher is the crucial fact of the whole work of education. It is you who have to transmit to the children some appreciation of the growth of the human spirit, some insight into our national traditions of liberty and fair play, into the material achievements of science, and into the wider problems set by racial and national divisions of mankind ; and somewhere through those lessons, through you, there must reach the children some of the " murmurs and the scents of the infinite sea."

It is not for you, fortunately, to undertake the political education of the children, but it is for you to see that if they have to hear of these things they hear both sides, and they hear them dispassionately, because you cannot prostitute your position to sectarian ends. The primary concern of those who have such a sacred trust as you have is the unfolding of the child's personality, and not the victory of party.

We all know that industrialism has its ugly side ; we all know we cannot maintain our population without strenuous competition, and we have a hard task in harmonising the claims of industry and the claims of an enlightened humanism. The harshest features of poverty we may hope to get rid of, and to provide against the worst crises of life, and perhaps in time to lift the level of our people ; but none of those things are of avail unless we can raise their character. Mr. Bertrand Russell wrote truly when he said : " It is true that poverty is a great evil, but it is not true that material prosperity is in itself a great good. If it is to have any real value to society, it must be made the means of advancement of those highest gifts that belong to the life of the mind "— and I would say the life of the soul.

In concluding, I would stress once more what I have said to you of the pre-eminent value in the teacher of character, for, if you look back upon your own childhood—as I look back upon mine—is it not a fact that all unconsciously we were the strongest moral judges of those set in authority over us ? It is not the clever teacher that we remember, or the man who taught us most—unless we gave our lives to scholarships ; what we remember is the man whose character all unconsciously impressed us, the man who was patient, who was honest, who was fair, and who brought into the performance of his daily task a spirit which, when we look back over the gulf of years, makes us feel even to-day, when we are faced, as we are faced day by day, with problems that test our character, that we should be almost afraid, as it were, to take the part that we know to be the less right one, because we feel somehow that that was the one thing that would not have met with the approval of him whom we knew all those years ago.

I will give you one sentence, if I may, which I read recently with great pleasure in a work by a schoolmaster, which seems to me to embody what I have been trying very feebly to express. He is speaking of the influence in after years of the schoolmaster on the pupil, and he speaks of the pupil, as an elderly man, looking back, in these words :

" Enlightened by the experience of fatherhood, they will see with a clear remembrance firmness in dealing with their moral faults or patience in dealing with their intellectual weakness, and, calling to mind the old schoolroom, they will think it was good for us to be there. For unknown to us therein were three tabernacles—one for us, one for our schoolmaster, and one for Him Who is the friend of all children and the Master of all schoolmasters."

If words like those can be said of us long after we have taught our last lesson or made our last speech, we shall not have done our work or lived our lives in vain, and the generations to come will rise up and call us blessed.

ON SOME GREAT MEN

MR. BONAR LAW

IN THE HOUSE OF COMMONS

13*th November*, 1923

THE House to-day meets under the shadow of a great loss—a public loss and a personal loss ; and I am sure it would not be the desire of Hon. Members to proceed to the ordinary business to-day without paying a tribute to the memory of a very great leader. Others will speak with greater eloquence than I can of his rare gifts in Parliament and in Council ; I should like, if I may, to speak to the House for a few minutes of some of the more personal aspects of the man. There is no doubt that Mr. Bonar Law gave his life for the country, just as much as if he had fallen in the Great War. The work he did during the War could only have been done by a man of great physical endurance and great intellectual capacity. It is difficult for all of us to realise what is meant by a man having served simultaneously in the War Cabinet—which sometimes used to sit for hours every day—as Chancellor of the Exchequer at a time when the Exchequer problems were more numerous and more difficult than they have ever been, and as Leader of the House of Commons—work which, however easily the business may be going, is always of a most exacting nature. Night after night when we had gone home the lights might have been seen burning in the room which I now occupy, where he would be working into the small hours of the morning on Departmental work, and nothing was more remarkable than the rapidity and accuracy with which he dealt with the difficult problems that came before him there. Mr. Keynes, no mean judge—and this is a great tribute from such a man—told me once that he often disagreed with Mr. Bonar Law, and that often he did not like his arguments, but he said that he was invariably right. I think there is nothing more remarkable than the general accuracy of his decisions at the Exchequer during the time that I had the honour of working so intimately with him, and the way in which, over a great matter such as the War Loan, he took a strong stand against a unanimous expert opinion, and proved himself by the results to have been in the right.

But hard as the work was, he never complained, and he was always full of kindness. He was always willing to let others have the credit for what was done. If the history of the time ever comes to be written, it can be proved that perhaps he did greater service in preventing the doing of things which it was wiser not to do, rather than in initiating things which ought to have been done.

The courage that he showed in his work was equally striking in other aspects. I remember on the 23rd March, 1918, when men's hearts were failing, he remained confident. He told me at the time that nothing could shake his unquenchable faith in the British soldier. It was the same with regard to air raids. I can see him now, with his family around him—and he was never happy at these times unless they were around him—sitting in the middle of them, working away, with the deafening noise outside, paying not the slightest attention to it, and the only time that I remember when he failed to work during an air raid was when one of his children was absent, and was reported to be making her way to Downing Street from some other part of London, and we lost Mr. Bonar Law, and we discovered that he had wandered out in his slippers on to the Horse Guards' Parade, in the middle of a heavy barrage, to look for his own child.

He had few illusions, and he was of a critical temperament, and yet with that I have never heard him say a single bitter, unkind or unfair word about a living soul. He looked for the best side in everybody, and if occasionally I may have said something to him hasty in criticism of this or that individual, he never would acknowledge it, but he immediately countered me by pointing to one of his good points. Like many men, he was changed by the War. He

LORD CURZON

23rd March, 1925

I HOPE, Sir, with the permission of the House, to make a few observations on the loss the Government and the country have sustained by the death of one of the greatest men and the most vivid personalities of this generation. I do so before this House in the knowledge that there are few here who can remember him in his earlier years, when, as a young man, he was a distinguished Member of this House, and one to whose future everyone looked forward with hope and with confidence. But I am particularly anxious, in a case like this, to try to give Members of the House some impression of the man himself, what lay behind, and what was the real man, which has been somewhat obscured in more recent years when he had withdrawn more from debates and from appearances in public.

It is difficult for us, who knew Lord Curzon after great honours had come to him, earned during a long life of service, to realise that he started many years ago with few advantages except his natural abilities and such advantages as might have accrued to him from belonging to a noble family. He was, in many senses of the word, a self-made man, because it was his natural ability, his fierce industry and his courage which made him, from an early period of life, map out the scheme of what he would do. He was the architect of his own fortune; he made his own friends; and he qualified himself for the great tasks of his life, not only by ceaseless study from early years, but by travel in what were then comparatively unknown parts of the world, by books, and by consorting with men of all kinds and in all countries.

His interests were exceptionally wide, and he proceeded to make himself a master of every subject in which his keen mind took an interest. So it is that the death of one primarily known to us as a statesman and a politician leaves more gaps in the public life of this country than would be the case with almost any other living man. As a student of the classics, a deep student of history, of pictures and of archaeology, his loss will be felt as much among the Trustees of the British Museum and the Trustees of the National Gallery as in the Cabinet, and his loss will perhaps be greatest in that Oxford that he loved so much. Oxford, as we know, whispering from her towers the last enchantments of the Middle Ages, spoke to him as she speaks to all her sons who have ears to hear, and to him perhaps more than most. Especially so, I think, because one of the keys to Lord Curzon's life is to remember that his roots had struck deep into pre-industrial England, and it is from an early England that he drew the sources of his strength. So it was that he had, possibly, less acquaintance with and interest in many of these strange currents of modern life in England, his mind turning naturally more to England in foreign and Imperial politics ; and yet—let there be no misunderstanding here—no proposal that could be made for the betterment of our people at home was welcomed more eagerly than by him, in very much the same spirit that it would have been welcomed by young England in the days of Disraeli's youth, of which period, in many ways, he seemed to be, even to-day, a member.

His learning, the learning of years, and the natural aptitude which he had, gave him a power of natural expression, whether in writing or in speech, that would have been remarkable at any time. Perhaps the most remarkable feature of it was that, great as it appeared to us when we heard him speaking in either this House or in another place, his quickness of mind was such that it was no less great when impromptu and without notice. The subject-matter and the humour bubbled up afresh and at a moment's notice.

With that equipment and that training, and with the training he obtained in this House, it is little wonder that he was able to enter upon one of the greatest phases of his life's work in India at so early an age for one occupying a position of such immense authority. There is no doubt that while he has always been a man whose heart and soul were for England and the Empire, yet his best friends would own that it was India and the East that held his imagination from his early youth until the end of his life. He regarded the presence of the Englishman in India as the presence of a man with a mission, and he regarded him as the servant of our country on a sacred mission. He never flinched from those high ideals and earnest endeavours, and, in spite of all, he held the scales of justice even in that great country.

But there, just as in his life afterwards, and in his political life, while he never sought popularity, he was always grateful for appreciation. He was, it is true, exacting towards others, and he demanded a very high standard, but he was not nearly as exacting towards others as he was towards himself. The standard that he demanded from others he demanded in a triple measure from himself.

But these things I have said are well known, and they may be found in biographies, and I want, if I may, for a few minutes to try to look a little more under the surface. Lord Curzon was a man who erected a façade about himself, and a façade which deceived many people and was the product of a natural shyness, an intense and exquisite sensitiveness. It is no uncommon thing, as each of us may know in our own lives and moving amongst the men we know, that human beings in this world who suffer from sensitiveness do put something between themselves and their fellow-men to ward off the shafts which they dread; yet underneath there beats the kindest, warmest human heart.

There was a nature, contrary to what many might believe who did not know him, of the uttermost simplicity—the eternal boy lived in him until the last week of his life. He was the soul of loyalty to his colleagues, he bore no grudges in political life, he pursued a straight course; and all this in the face of daily and constant physical suffering. Of that many knew nothing, because it was a thing of which he never spoke. But I have seen him at the Cabinet, I have seen him at a dinner party, and if he were not able to have the necessary cushions to support his back, his suffering would be as the suffering of a man on the rack, and that he fought against day by day. When we look back upon him, I feel that what Lord Rosebery said of William Pitt is so true of him, that whatever men may feel about his life or his acts, they must be agreed that England had in this generation no more patriotic spirit, none more intrepid, and none more pure.

I want before I sit down to say one or two things that no one but I can say. A Prime Minister sees human nature bared to the bone, and it was my chance to see him twice when he suffered great disappointment—the time when I was preferred to him as Prime Minister, and the time when I had to tell him that he could render greater service to the country as Chairman of the Committee of Imperial Defence than in the Foreign Office. Each of those occasions was a profound and bitter disappointment to him, but never for one moment when he had faced the facts did he show by word, look or innuendo, or by any reference to the subject afterwards, that he was dissatisfied. He bore no grudge, and he pursued no other course than the one I expected of him, of doing his duty where it was decided that he could best render service.

I felt on both those occasions that I had seen in him, in that strange alloy which we call human nature, a vein of the purest gold. He died as he would have desired, and as we should all desire to die, in harness, a harness put on himself in youth and worn triumphantly through a long life, a harness which he never cast off until his feet had entered the river. It may well be when we look back on that life of devoted service to his country, and of a perpetual triumph of the spirit over the flesh, that in some places in this earth, early on that Friday morning, may have been heard the faint echoes of the trumpets that sounded for him on the other side.

LORD MILNER AND ARNOLD TOYNBEE

FROM A SPEECH AT OXFORD

15th May, 1925

I FEEL to-night that I cannot do better than say something to you about what Lord Milner stood for in this world of ours, what he has meant for his generation, and what the message is that he has for our party and for the whole Empire. It is thirty years since Lord Milner paid a great tribute to another Oxford man, a friend of his own, whose name I hope is not forgotten yet in Oxford. I mean Arnold Toynbee. Arnold Toynbee was a product of his generation, but he was more than that. He lived at a time when the industrial revolution of this country had so far succeeded that those who worked with their hands were being more vocal and more clamant about their position, and what they conceived to be their rights, and the duties of those whose lot in life was more fortunate, and at a time when the consciences of the well-to-do were beginning to be stimulated and to react to the touch of those who in the middle of the last century had been but voices in the desert. Toynbee, by his friendship, by his own ardent nature, and by the social experiment that he made in his short life, in supporting the movement [1] for university settlements put in the poorer quarters of our great towns, and by stimulating interest throughout the educated and the more fortunate classes in what was going on around them in worlds they knew but little, was more than any-one perhaps of his generation the pioneer of much that has happened since and the father of movements begun in but a small way, but which have helped to change the whole outlook of the English people in the matter of social life and social reform. It was that devotion, that unselfish devotion, of Toynbee and his friends to social service that captivated Milner in his youth and that, in spite of all the vicissitudes, political and others, that attended his life, remained with him as an abiding inspiration; and, indeed, it is from that inspiration that we who are here to-night as members of a revivified and triumphant Conservative Party draw our breath and have our being.

It is difficult to realise the change that has come over the thought of our country in the course of one short or two short generations. When Milner came up to Oxford the old *laissez-faire* school still reigned unchallenged in all matters, social and economic. If I may quote his own words, he said : " All the recognised authorities were orthodox economists of the old school, but within ten years the few men who still held the doctrines in their extreme rigidity had

[1] The original inspiration of the movement was given by the late Canon Barnett and Mrs. (now Dame Henrietta) Barnett, who founded Toynbee Hall.

come to be regarded as curiosities." And Milner said himself, in answer to a question that was often asked at that time, " Was Arnold Toynbee a Socialist ? "—and his words, I think, are full of wisdom, applicable to the present day even more than they were applicable to the day when he said them : " If by Socialism you mean collectivism, the abolition of individual property, or if you mean social democracy, the paternal government of an omnipotent, all-absorbing State, then Toynbee was certainly no Socialist. But on the other hand, he was convinced of the necessity of social reorganisation. The Industrial Revolution had shattered the old social system. It had left the industrial life of this and the other great civilised countries of the West in a state of profound disorder, and society, left to itself, could not right itself. Salvation would only come through deliberate corporate effort, inspired by moral issues, though guided by the scientific study of economic laws." And I do not think that that is any bad definition of the ideals which we to-day are working for.

Going back once more for a moment to the time of Toynbee and when Milner was a young man, there were published some other books which I daresay are unknown to this generation, but the contents of which and the ideas of which ran through all thoughtful England like a heath fire, and those were the revelations which appeared in General Booth's book on *Darkest England*, and the scientific investigation or poverty by Mr. Charles Booth, who devoted a remarkable natural ability, great wealth, and tireless industry for the first time to the tabulation of facts regarding the condition of the people under our industrial system in our great towns—books which have been for years after their publication a mine of wealth of knowledge to all who sought to do work, in whatever capacity, in trying to amend the social conditions of our people.

Much has been done since those days. Much has been done to grapple with the problems of unemployment, with the problems of health and of housing, which the reformers of that generation would have rejoiced to see, more perhaps than many of them could have hoped to see. But yet we are not satisfied, and we have to take stock at the present time, and we have to ask ourselves if those great men who preceded us would have been satisfied to rest now in the conditions in which we find ourselves. Now Lord Milner, with his highly trained intellect, waged war against twin evils which always struck his mind perhaps more than any others—inefficiency and waste—and his whole life was a protest against these things. All the efforts that he made in inspiring other public men in the course of their work were directed to combat those evils. He had no patience with what we in England are often only too proud of—our capacity for muddling through. He had no sympathy with muddling, whether you got through or not.

But people who did not know him often failed to realise the profound humanity that lay underneath that shy and reserved exterior, and which accompanied—and profound humanity does not always accompany—great gifts of intellect. No one who worked with Lord Milner could ever forget this—that, in every social problem that he approached, whether at home or abroad, the question he always asked himself was this : " How can we help those who have to carry the burden and heat of the day, and how will what we propose to do affect those who have to work with their hands for their daily bread ? " He believed that the right way towards social prosperity and the reorganisation of this country lay through the scientific organisation of our productive power, and it was his belief in the practicability of accomplishing this that made him always turn a deaf ear to those who argued that the first necessity of bringing about capacities for industrial production and competition was a lowering of wages and standards of life. He was always opposed to that. But it is probable that with his great intellectual gifts, and with a certain intellectual detachment, and from not having mixed for long or very freely with all classes of people in this country, he failed perhaps to realise the natural, dare I say obtuseness ? of his fellow-countrymen—or, let us say, the difficulties owing to the English temperament of giving effect speedily to what he desired.

I think that in what he desired to do he was very

largely right, because, whether you look at home or throughout the Dominions and Colonies, there is no doubt there is an immense amount to do in the way of scientific development and of co-ordination— much as I dislike that word co-ordination—both with regard to improving the productive capacity of the Empire, and no less with regard to co-ordinating, which is equally important, the scientific work which has been done in different parts of the Empire with regard not only to production, but with regard to health and sanitation. We have allowed our Empire for too long to proceed on haphazard lines. He felt that we were handicapped as against the world, compared with what we ought to be, by an unnecessary economic backwardness prevailing in so many parts of the Empire. To use his own words, he said " that such backwardness is a discredit alike to our generosity and to our intelligence."

. . . .

The word Imperialism still has to many people in this country a rather sinister meaning. They associate with it—wrongly in my view and in your view—the idea of exploitation, of riding roughshod over the world, of jingoism and of selfishness in public policy. It was not that to Lord Milner, and it is not that to us. It is rather this—the spreading throughout such parts of the world as we control, or in which we have influence, of all those ideas of law, order, and justice which we believe to be peculiar to our own race. It is to help people who belong to a backward civilisation, wisely to raise them in the scale of civilisation—an extraordinarily difficult task, and one which needs wisdom for its consummation. There is no country in the world upon whom that task has been imposed to the same degree as our own country, and it is undoubtedly by the way in which we fulfil that task that we shall be judged at the bar of history, not perhaps so much to-day, but by those who come after us of our own blood.

We have made a start, so far as our own Empire is concerned, by setting up an Imperial Economic Committee to try to bring about still closer bonds commercially between the Dominions and the Mother Country. All attempts to-day must be to a certain extent tentative. But I am quite convinced, having regard to the sentiment throughout the Empire, that we are approaching along a line that affords the best chance of our laying the foundation to-day for something upon which a far mightier edifice may be built in years to come. I am convinced, too, we are only at the beginning of what can be done by intelligent co-operation of the Mother Country with the Colonies and the Empire in developing them for the benefit not only of themselves and ourselves, but of the Empire as a whole.

It is upon that point I want to say a few words to you in Oxford. I often used to wonder whether it was possible that this world of ours had existed an unknown period, and mankind had struggled on in its upward course through countless generations of toil and tribulation, so that a few of us might be able to come to Oxford and Cambridge to enjoy ourselves and to pass on, taking the cream of civilisation. It always seemed to me that if all we have to show for what humanity is suffering was a little privileged generation in a corner of the world like this, the whole thing, creation and evolution, became something puny and ridiculous. It seemed to me that for us who have the enormous inestimable privilege of being born into this country in positions where we can come here, and where to a certain extent we choose what we do in the world, that really after all that has been given to us, and after all that we have enjoyed, and with a vivid recollection of what this world has passed through within the last ten years, there is nothing else for this generation to do than to devote itself as no generation has done in the past to the betterment of its millions of people who have not got our advantages.

We have, or we can have if we like, what the whole of this country is crying out for to-day, and that is education. Never was the need for educated men in each country of the Empire greater than it is to-day. The greatest loss that the war has imposed on this country is the loss of a whole generation of men who to-day would be between the ages of thirty and forty-five, able to carry on and take over the big jobs ; and they were wiped out. Where many years ago there were men to be reckoned in dozens to take over responsible and arduous duties throughout the

Empire and at home, now there are but handfuls, and never was the call to service and the demand for service more clamant than to-day. Now there are many kinds of service for which you can offer yourself ; for those who have fitted themselves for it, if there is no immediate call for you into professions at home, think how the Empire needs you to-day to make the rough places smooth in all the corners of the world, to train and educate people lower than we are in the scale of civilisation, to go out to the great Dominions and help them in the problems set before them. And, apart from all those, what a field there is to-day for the best men that we can send to India, for this reason—for this and the next generation, the most difficult work in the Empire must necessarily be in that great country, work demanding sympathy, knowledge, courage, and intelligence of the highest order.

I hope it may never be said that in any part of the Empire when the call comes for workers, the one part where the call is most urgent, where the work is most difficult, and the future is most obscure, could be the one part where the call is not answered. If that should be the case it would be a proof of what I deny, but what some people maintain, that the courage, the initiative, and the spirit of adventure of our people, to which we owe the Empire and all that we are—that that spirit, if not dead, is dormant. I will never believe that.

Let me tell you at this point one story of Lord

Milner, which I expect will be new to most of you. I tell it to you, not only to show you, if you have any doubt, what manner of man he was, but to show you what the finest type of Englishman at his best can be ; the type that all of us would wish to emulate. Twenty-two years ago Lord Milner had completed about two years of work in the restoration of South Africa, one of the most difficult tasks to which any man had ever been called upon to devote himself, and, by confession on all hands, he had accomplished a work which it is doubtful if anyone else could have accomplished. His praise was in all men's mouths. He was a man who loved his own home in his own country, never so happy as when in England, and there came to him at that moment an offer from Lord Balfour to come home as Secretary of State for the Colonies, a task for which he was peculiarly fitted, and in every way he would have delighted in the work. He declined—and why ? He declined it because he knew that, in spite of the success he had achieved, there were coming years of the utmost difficulty in South Africa, years in which probably he would lose all the popularity he had won, years in which possibly his success might be turned into failure, and he said, " No, no, I am not going to go away from here and take the credit of accomplishments up to this point and leave someone else to come out now to face what must be years of difficulty and distress. I am going to see them through myself."

The public did not know that. That shows the finest temper, the finest spirit in which an Englishman could possibly do and face his work, and I would like to take to myself as an exemplar and a pattern that method of looking at my problems and facing my work. I would ask all of you, happy to have your lives before you, to keep a model of that kind ever present in your hearts and minds to be with you if you are ever called upon to face times of hardship and of difficulty. I make no apology to you when his loss is fresh, and I am sure is in all your hearts, and when it is weighing heavily on all of us who knew and loved him, for putting before an Oxford audience the inspiring example of one of her greatest sons, especially as the objects at which he aimed and the spirit in which he worked are the objects at which our party aims to-day, the spirit in which I hope and believe we work at a time like this, when the party to which we all belong is more united in its determination than it has ever been to follow in the steps of those who have set before everything the improvement of the material condition of our people, and of the whole of our Empire. Work to that end is to be achieved only by keeping in ourselves a bright and burning spiritual ideal, which alone can give us strength to perform the task to which we have set our hands.

LORD OXFORD

At the Guildhall
13*th May*, 1925

I PROPOSE to dwell, not on Lord Oxford the statesman, but on the Mr. Asquith whom we, in the House
of Commons, whether we agree with him or not,
have always respected and admired for a generation.
For many years, as a humble back-bencher, I had
my individuality, my hopes and my ambitions
trampled under foot by those marching legions of
which for so many years Mr. Asquith was the head.
But all through that time I recognised, as all of us
do, the stability of his character, the serenity of his
temper, his freedom from jealousies and enmities,
the magnitude of his mind and the plenitude of his
utterance. We felt that in him we had a master of
our tongue. In his speech he could be not only
sonorous, but, what does not always go with it,
luminous ; not only massive at times, but really
humorous. And he never supported his arguments
with any extraneous helps, such as Dr. Johnson
alluded to when he spoke of orators " who employ
laboured gesticulation and think that they can

impress themselves on audiences by rolling their eyes, puffing their cheeks, spreading abroad their arms, or stamping on the ground." There was with him always that reticence and reserve that belong essentially to the Roman and the Englishman rather than to the Greek and the Celt.

It is a curious thing that there was a Lord Oxford who preceded him by some two centuries, and if we look back on what was said about him by Swift, particularly, you get a not wholly imperfect picture of the Mr. Asquith whom we knew and respected so much. Listen to these few sentences, which, I think, might with very little change have been written to-day about Lord Oxford :

" Easy and disengaged in private conversation with such a weight of affairs upon his shoulders : of great learning, and as great a favourer and protector of it ; intrepid by nature, as well as by consciousness of his own integrity ; a despiser of money, a firm friend, and a placable enemy : sacrificing his justest resentment not only to the public good, but to the common intercession and acknowledgment. Yet with all these virtues "—here, I think, the truth will hold—" there is some mixture of human infirmity. His greatest admirers must confess his skill at cards and dice to be very low and superficial. Of horse-racing he is entirely ignorant."

I would like to finish on the note on which I began. My own admiration for Lord Oxford arose primarily from the admiration I have for his speeches, and I can recall three outstanding ones, very different in their kind, but which, I think, every old House of

Commons man will agree with me were instances of perfect speech. One was the speech Lord Oxford made on the death of Alfred Lyttelton. The second was the last speech he made in the House of Commons, a speech full of humour and Parliamentary skill, and one which led more than anything else directly to the fall of the late Government. Lastly, there was the great speech he delivered on 6th August, 1914, in which he put before this country and the world the principles of constitutional freedom as opposed to despotism in a manner in which they can never have been stated since the time of Edmund Burke.

He has taught us—those of us in the House of Commons and all students of politics to-day—not only to love our mother tongue more, if possible, than we have loved it in the past, but also the possibilities of that tongue when it is properly used. He has given us an example by which some of us, if we apply ourselves, and if we have the ability to profit by his example, may some day be able ourselves to speak English.

ON THE NATION AND THE CHURCHES

RELIGION AND POLITICS

FROM A SPEECH AT THE LANGHAM HOTEL
11*th February*, 1926

MANY people, I fear, to-day fail to realise the very critical character of the period through which the world is passing. There is nothing the country needs so much as another Wesley or Whitefield. Those spiritual movements, such as occurred in the eighteenth century, led largely by Wesley, have come up from time to time in the history of the human race. Their spirit is always the same, though the form is different. Had Wesley been born four centuries earlier, he would have been Wesley just the same, but he would have worn a rough robe girded with a cord and have founded a great body of preaching friars. I confess I am not sure, if a Wesley or a St. Francis arose to-day, that to found a body of preaching friars would not be the best thing they could do for the world. To-day the world seems more irreligious than it has ever been in the Christian era. Irresponsible pleasure-seeking and prodigal luxury abound ; church-going has lost the hold it had in our childhood ; and candidates for the Ministry are less in number than in years past. But I believe this condition of affairs will pass. The side of Christianity which takes into view all kinds of activities for the social betterment of the people is the side which most appeals to the present generation. Undoubtedly there is as much philanthropic and altruistic work done by all kinds of people as has ever been done.

I find the study of the various types in the House of Commons a very interesting occupation. I find there, especially among the Labour Party, many men who fifty years ago would inevitably have gone into the Christian Ministry. They have been drawn into political life from a deep desire to help the people. Such men are common in all parties to-day. These are facts which relieve the darkness of the outlook. Things will change again. We must not let ourselves imagine, amidst the changes of the day, though the very foundations are cracking, that the things we hold most precious are going to pass away. I certainly agree with many observers that since the war the manifest forces of Satan have been more conspicuously at large. But the very manifestation of these forces is calling other forces into the field.

On this account I feel it to be so important that a Church like yours should send its quota of young men into politics to-day. Political work is of enormous importance at this time. We do not all realise in what a changed world we are living. Superficially it is a frivolous world, full of " jazzing " and pre-occupation with pleasure, but under the surface it is intensely serious. I believe the electorate is intensely anxious to listen to men who have sincerely at heart the uplifting of the nation.

Many of those who seem to be running most wild in their political views are men who have been led astray by insufficient education or experience, but are truly desirous of bettering their country. Therefore, I believe that men who will sincerely and honestly embrace political life with the idea of helping the community (no matter to what party they belong), are wanted in these days. This, coupled with the desire of service, will defeat the menacing forces which threaten us. If, in consequence of words spoken this night, some of the young men connected with the Wesleyan Methodist Church feel the call to political work, it will be of great advantage to the Commonwealth, for the political career properly viewed is really a kind of Ministry.

THE CHURCH ARMY

AT A MEETING OF THE CHURCH ARMY IN QUEEN'S HALL

7th May, 1925

I AM afraid I have been talking too much during the last few days. On Tuesday I was talking to newspaper men about truth ; on Wednesday I was talking to artists about beauty ; and now I am at this great meeting, the note of which and the key to which are goodness, truth and beauty, which surely make a perfect trinity, since no man can be leading the ideal life unless he has these things combined in unity in himself.

I think that perhaps we are awakening more and more to the deeper spiritual impulses and to their importance in the life of the country. When we read (or used to read) history, we find a great deal one hundred and two hundred years ago about politics, kings and battles, but very little about a man called John Wesley. Yet, as the years go by, historians have begun to say that it was the lives of men like Wesley and Whitefield, and what they taught the people of this country, that really were the significant factors in moulding the character of the people and of the leaders of the people, and that it is largely owing to the spirit which they, and men like them, breathed throughout England, that the immense impetus was given to the reforms—social and religious—which took place in the country during the last century, and which helped, in spite of a thousand difficulties and evil things on the other side, to make the rough path smoother and to kindle afresh the Divine spark in the hearts of men.

So, when the history of the nineteenth century comes to be written, I believe there will stand out the names of two men, William Booth and Wilson Carlile, who represent the spiritual revolt voiced before them by Ruskin and many another against the ugliness of life, and its sin and its blind devotion to nothing but material progress. I have always thought that if Mr. Carlile had lived many centuries ago, instead of to-day, he would have been one of the first of the Franciscans. He has shown the country what the Church of England can do, and there has been no risk for him of sharing the fate that fell to John Wesley, and of another schism being unnecessarily caused among the people of God in this land.

The record of the Church Army is a modern chapter in the Acts of the Apostles, and its work is as inspired as anything of which we read in the sacred Scriptures. The Church Army is a living testimony of what a life of Divine love can mean in the hearts of ordinary men and women. Whatever controversies rage—doctrinal, theological—among men who profess religion, they go on their way and combine to give a glorious demonstration of personal devotion in the service of men.

The activities of the Church Army are innumerable—in emigration, recreation and good, honest mirth, preaching—but, above all, coming to the rescue of fallen humanity. When I think of this I cannot help feeling, as I look around this room, that there can be no life on this earth in which men may be more sure to find real happiness than in this life of perpetual self-sacrifice. We may look in vain in the faces of those whose life is one constant search for illusive pleasures to see the radiant expressions which I have noticed in all parts of this great audience.

The work of many of you is not only among the poor and unfortunate, but among men and women who are the broken results of life in this age—men and women who, in many cases, have lost not only work and health, but what is far more difficult to make good, their spirit, temper, *morale*, courage and faith. Yet the Church Army goes out to its work preserving that spirit of health and happiness which is its motto. It shows that the more men will give their lives to service and the more impossible the tasks they try to achieve, the more is the grace given them in that fight, the brighter their faith burns, and the more they are able to radiate among those with whom they work that spirit of confidence, hope and happiness which the world needs and desires so much. I have watched your work with the deepest and most heartfelt sympathy and admiration, and I only wish that I personally was competent to do it. You look in the most unlikely places for that spark of the Divine which exists in every human soul. You search until you find it, and then you blow on it with the spirit of love till you have blown it into a flame, however feeble ; and so you have one more to testify to the eternal truth that love alone in this world is the conqueror, and that by love alone can the nations be brought into the paths of peace, and that to pursue and attain love is the one thing needful.

CHRISTIAN IDEALS

AT THE NATIONAL FREE CHURCH CONFERENCE
12th March, 1925

YOU have taken the opportunity to waylay and entrap a singularly busy man on his way to make an ordinary political speech, and you have brought him to speak to you this afternoon for a few moments before an assembly distinctly representative of a great deal of the religious movement and religious thought of the country. Curiously enough, this is the first occasion, I think, on which I have ever addressed a body directly concerned with any of the churches. I have in the past always been reluctant to speak at those gatherings, possibly from the Englishman's fear of saying in the excitement of a public audience more than he really felt or really believed, knowing as a public man the temptation of winning easy applause by saying comfortable things, by saying things that perhaps are an exaggeration of what one really feels oneself, with the inevitable result, so often seen, that the more popular one becomes as a speaker the greater is the tendency to spiritual atrophy in the individual.

Now, the first thought that naturally occurs to me at an assembly of this kind is the difference between the work that lies before the politician and the work that lies before the Christian minister. I represent here and in this visit the State ; you represent the Church. You are the Guelphs and I am the Ghibellines, and there are some marked points of difference that it may help us to dwell upon for a few moments. But, tempting as the theme would be, I have neither the time to-day nor even the inclination to dwell on the struggles, the secular struggles, that have taken place between Church and State, and the great part played in these struggles and the development of life in our country by the Free Churches of England.

In many ways, in that struggle, I think we may say that we have often been in religious life far in advance, as we ought to be, of political life. For, while it is true that in distant ages long past representatives of Christianity tried to drive mankind into their fold by stern measures, by execution and by fire, we have left those things far behind us, and it has remained in the last century for wild and extreme men in some parts of the world to apply, in trying to make mankind believe their political doctrines, weapons which have been given up by the Christian for more centuries than I like to think of.

I, in my capacity as a politician, have to deal with mankind in the mass. You, in the life of your churches, have to deal with the individual ; and the difference lies in this, that the problems of life come to us wholesale, as it were. We have columns of figures before us of unemployment, for instance. You don't trouble about columns of figures, but you all, in your lives and in your ministry, when you think of unemployment, think of the man and the woman and the child ; and while we are devising methods of helping, so far as we can, you have vividly before you the daily increase in the hopelessness, the daily increase in the lack of skill, the daily increase in the lack of *morale*. It may well be that you feel, as you must at times, impatient with those, to whatever party they may belong, who are attempting to govern this great country, for their inability at once to find something that will alleviate the troubles from which our people suffer to-day.

There is another aspect of this. Parliament represents all the citizens in a way that religious bodies cannot. Your membership is voluntary. We are all born members of the State, and you have an excluding discipline which we in politics have not. You can supply selective tests both to your members and to your ministers—tests of character, tests of knowledge, tests of belief—and you can make them obedient to a rule of life. I can do none of these things and, indeed, I have only to try to do the best I can with the tools I have, which means to work the existing institutions of the country so far as I conceive it to the best advantage of the multitudinous interests of her citizens. Then again, while you have, and all churches have, their rule of life, you cannot say that there is any definite code laid down for all political parties. My party have no political bible. Possibly you might find our ideals best expressed in one of Disraeli's novels, but I have no power to make people read them, and I have no power to compel them to belief.

It would ill become me to say what may be the bible, if there be such a book, of the Liberal Party. The party that can claim more than any of the others to have a religious code to-day is the Labour Party, because they still have the Marxian *Capital*, but, as a matter of fact, that book has been subject, as other books, to the higher criticism for some years past, and what will happen when the results of higher criticism percolate to the lower intelligence I have little idea.

There is yet a third difference : we of the State do possess—to a certain extent—the power of compulsion. We can enforce the law, and we can enforce it upon the unwilling. But the sense of the State in the minds and hearts of most men is still feeble and undeveloped. The State wears an extravagant guise to them, and they are apt to serve it with a grudging assent. In a supreme crisis men will lay down their lives for it, but they don't lay down their lives conscientiously so much for what we call the State as for the country behind it. We in politics—let me say politicians—even at the moment of the greatest popularity cannot, and perhaps ought not to, command the love and enthusiasm that the Church, if it is to be the instrument it might be, can command, and ought to command, from her sons and daughters.

But after looking for a few minutes at the obvious differences, one comes to the more congenial topic of how we are able to help one another.

What can the Christian Church do for the State ? Now, here again we have many voices speaking to us to-day, and, while it would ill become me to say anything on any difference of opinion that may exist among you, I think I may take two typical voices in the Church of England which do express to-day two different lines of thought, and which yet seem to me to converge if you only go down underneath the surface. The Bishop of Durham and the Bishop of Manchester represent two very different schools of political thought. The Bishop of Durham stresses the individual appeal of the Gospel, and the Bishop of Manchester the social application of the Christian message. Those are two sides of the same thing, and I think we ought to look at both sides at once.

To my mind, the distinctive Christian motive is the individual transformation of character. The making of that character reacts on the national life, and I think the Bishop of Durham quite truly pointed out that, so little effect, looking at it historically, has the quality of the social order had on individual morality with all varieties of social organisation, that sometimes even the worst periods of history have been found compatible with and to co-exist with the very finest development of the Christian character. And I venture to agree with him when he stressed what I spoke of in my first sentence, the danger of people thinking they can satisfy their consciences by talking at large on sacred subjects and on general amelioration, and amelioration to be brought about by social improvements, unless at the same time they never lose sight of the fact that you must come back ultimately and all the time to the individual ; and that you must not let the joy of beautiful visions or discussions on dogma or any other things make you forget that it is the ethic, it is the life, it is the transformation of life, that is the thing which really matters. Work up from that to the other, and don't try to work down from the other to that.

He also reminds us of what I think many need to be reminded, that this world is a much harder place to live in and do your duty in than we sometimes care to remember. It is so much more comfortable to make easy speeches. Browning has said, " How very hard it is to be a Christian," and he never said anything more true. But, of course, this does not express the whole truth. It is quite true that you cannot identify Our Lord with any academic theory or school, Tory, Manchester or Marxian, and when we try to do that I think we make a profound error ; yet, living in this world, the bodies of Christian people, united by a common ideal, have to act not only as individuals but as corporate bodies and communities, and it is when they come to act in that way that their real difficulties, it seems to me, begin.

This is a point which the Bishop of Manchester stresses, and, if I may say so with respect, quite rightly. His desire is to see the Christian Churches really influencing public life in this country, not taking sides, but raising the standard of the country's ideals, criticising, judging, with Christian charity where possible, but criticising and judging, that we may be told where we fall short of the highest ideals in trying to apply political and social remedies in this country.

It is quite right to tell us, and to tell us emphatically, that the Christian Churches should give themselves to helping in the elevation of the social condition of the country, and not be satisfied with things as they are. You have the double message, and I am sure you have it in all your Churches through your different teachers and different types —the cultivation of the spiritual life of the individual, the regeneration of the mass through the individual, and the reaction of the regenerated mass on the country at large.

That should be the process, and I think that in these days we all of us want, perhaps more than anything, and more than at any time, to be bound lightly and loosely to the luxuries and the good things of this world. We cannot all of us embrace poverty as St. Francis did, but we all know the difference between the man who cherishes the treasures of this world and the man who sits lightly to them, and it is only by sitting lightly to them that you have the right to say much that wants saying in these days ; for it is only in that way that you can hope to influence those amongst whom you work, rich and poor alike. It is a spirit essential to-day in the present conditions of our country, and I believe and recognise with joy that it is more common to-day amongst those who are directly relieved from poverty than it was in the years before the War.

People often say that this is a materialistic age. There is much truth in that, but I do feel, too, that there has never been an age in which there are more people struggling, some with more success and some with less, to live to the highest ideals that are in them, and doing something to help to better the moral and the physical conditions of the people among whom they live. And it is only natural, in a time when you have active and strong the spirit of things that make for good, that you have co-existent with it the spirit that makes for evil no less active and strong. I think that that is possibly one of the reasons why you see the great contrast that you do see to-day, and that while it is true that there is throughout Europe a great deal of gross and crass materialism, you have at the same time all over Europe eager souls who are struggling to impress themselves on their day, to improve themselves and to improve the world.

Now, in that struggle we all have to take our part. That struggle exists everywhere, and is round us every day, and in that struggle what help to the country can the churches of England give ? They stand reminders day by day of that truth in which they have been born—to teach us to shun the luxury that divides us so much from one another, to spread the education that ought to unite us, to supply us with an inspiration to sustain us. In ways such as this the churches of England can hold up the right arms of the politicians of England and join in the common work of making the crooked paths a little straighter and the rough places a little smoother for our own people.

I think it is well in an assembly like this to remember one other thing. Some people talk as though Christianity had done its work in the world —a singular lack of imagination in that remark, seeing that the work has hardly yet been begun. There is not one of you in an assembly like this who has not known at one time of your life a character which can only have been formed on the model of Our Lord and Master—some man, some woman, it may have been someone among the highly educated and fortunate in the world, it may have been a working person. But we have all known, at one time or another, such a one, and it has been a great help to us in our pilgrimage through life to look to that example and to walk to some extent in the light that they cast on their path as they passed along. Now churches may rise and churches may fall, but the influence of lives like that will go on for ever, and it is through the light of such lives that the redemption of this world will ultimately come ; for they will survive persecution, and derision, and coldness, and apathy. We shall never see those times, nor our children, nor our children's children ; but it will be by the succession of such lives as I have endeavoured to depict that some day the Kingdom of Heaven will come on earth. If we cannot hold fast in the most difficult times to an ideal of that kind, we shall find that we shall be suffocated in the daily toil which most of us have to undergo, and as a people we shall go down and perish for lack of vision.

ON THE EMPIRE

EMPIRE DAY MESSAGE, 1925

TWENTY years ago Empire Day was first celebrated throughout His Majesty's Dominions. Twenty years hence the Prime Minister of Great Britain may be able to make his voice heard, not only—as I am to-day—to listeners in the home country, but to men, women and children in all parts of the Empire. We, too, in Great Britain may listen to Empire Day messages spoken by the Dominion Prime Ministers and by leaders of the Crown Colonies and the Dependencies. Such a consummation of scientific progress makes a strong appeal to the imagination. The direct interchange of speech would bring home to every dweller under the Flag a vivid sense of the unity of the British Empire. Yet, to my mind, the existence of that unity to-day, and in all past days since the foundations of our Empire were laid, is a far more impressive phenomenon.

Our Empire grew from the adventurous spirit of our fathers. They went forth, urged by the love of adventure, by the passion for discovery, by the desire for a freer life in new countries. Wherever they went, they carried with them the traditions, the habits, the ideals of their Mother Country. Wherever they settled they planted a new homeland. And though mountains and the waste of seas divided them, they never lost that golden thread of the spirit which drew their thoughts back to the land of their birth. Even their children, and their children's children, to whom Great Britain was no more than a name, a vision, spoke of it always as Home. In this sense of kinship, the Empire finds its brightest glory and its most essential strength. The Empires of old were created by military conquest and sustained by military domination. They were Empires of subject races governed by a central power. Our Empire is so different from these that we must give the word Empire a new meaning, or use instead of it the title of Commonwealth of British Nations. The great Dominions are free self-governing States ; in their freedom they render unshakeable allegiance to the Throne. The ties that bind them to each other and to us are, in the eloquent words of Burke, " light as air, but strong as links of iron." Each is a daughter in her mother's house, and mistress in her own.

We British are supposed to be a dull, unimaginative race. But I am sure that none among us can think upon this Commonwealth of British nations, which men and women of our own race have created, without a stirring of our deepest feelings. If anyone should ask for proof that the unity of the Empire is a reality, let him cast his mind back to the hour when the living structure of Empire was put to the supreme test. When war came the response of the Empire was instant, spontaneous and whole-hearted. You and I can never forget how our hearts were uplifted by the messages which came, in those critical days of August 1914, from the great Dominions ; and not only from them, but also from India and the Colonies which were still under our rule. The Empire came through the ordeal of a long and exhausting war, strengthened, confirmed in its loyalty.

To-day our minds are engrossed with the problems of restoration after war. What brighter hope have we, in the solution of these formidable problems, than our intimate union with countries of great achievement and still greater potentialities ? These are not times when we can afford to belittle the material side of partnership in Empire. If we, in these crowded industrial islands, can serve the interests of newer countries ; and if they, in turn, with their fertile spaces and unlimited natural resources, can serve our interests, we are more than justified in making common cause with them in repairing the waste of war. This sense of a common purpose, this desire for mutual aid, gives a practical touch to the ideal of Empire as a family of nations. When each member of the family seeks to give its aid, freely, ungrudgingly, for the good of all, the fabric of the Commonwealth is more and more closely knit.

It is the task of statesmen in this country and throughout the Empire to devise the ways and means by which the progress of the British family may be directed and encouraged. Each one of us, from the highest to the lowest, has nevertheless an individual share in this great responsibility. The Empire is not only our master hope ; it is our greatest heritage, the widest opportunity for patriotic service. It is something infinitely precious which we hold in trust from our forefathers and for our children. To be worthy of that trust, we cannot be merely passive admirers of its achievement and its promise. We must all, in our several degrees, be active learners in the school of Empire. Over and over again our friends from overseas complain of the ignorance displayed by people at home regarding the Dominions, Colonies, and Dependencies. I think that our ardent and friendly critics are inclined to overlook the difficulty which our busy folk experience in gathering clear and comprehensive knowledge of all parts of the Empire. It is no little task for people to know all that goes on in our great Dominions, to understand the problems confronting our Crown Colonies, and to enter into the life of the Indian Empire and the Dependencies, where a handful of our countrymen labour for the benefit of millions of native races in all stages of culture. But the difficulty of the duty is no reason why we should neglect it. Rather is it a stimulus to exert ourselves to widen our knowledge of the countries and the nations which share with us in the obligations of Empire.

I feel sure, however, that since the opening of the Empire Exhibition at Wembley last year, this affectionate grumble from our brothers overseas has lost much of its point. The Exhibition enabled, and still enables, our people to learn in a few days much which could not otherwise be appreciated save by a tour of the Empire. No one can adequately measure the value of such a demonstration of the arts and industries of the Commonwealth of British nations. In more than one sense the Empire came home to us at Wembley. There are many ways, apart from such exhibitions, by which we can study our Empire at second hand. But nothing, to my mind, can prove so enlightening as personal visits overseas, and personal intercourse with dwellers in our Dominions and Colonies. We are accustomed to look upon the oceans as dividing us from our brothers and sisters in the Imperial family. I prefer to regard the seas as highways which unite us. The progress of communication has made it possible for us to visit Canada, South Africa, Egypt, the West Indies, and other portions of the Empire with less trouble and expense than our fathers incurred in making their Continental tours. It should be the ambition of all of us to pay at least one visit, however brief, to Britain overseas.

Apart from that, we can do something to foster the interchange of visits for educative ends. The Empire Parliamentary Association has done invaluable work in bringing together legislators from different parts of the Empire. Recently a number of Australian school children visited Great Britain, and public interest was awakened to the value of similar visits by our children to the Dominions. All such movements deserve the fullest encouragement.

Empire Day affords us an opportunity for joining with other parts of the Empire in expressing our common pride in our Imperial heritage, and our common determination to build worthily upon the foundations which the great Empire-builders so well and truly laid. If I were to attempt to crystallise its message in a phrase, I might take the words, " Know Thyself," in which the ancients expressed the duty of the individual man, and widen it to embrace the duty of the British citizen of to-day— " Know Your Empire."

DEMOCRACY AND THE EMPIRE

From a Speech to the Junior Imperial League
3rd May, 1924

YOUR generosity in your reception of me to-night is no less than the generosity which you showed me when, immediately after defeat in the country, and before my leadership had been ratified by the party in London, you asked me to come here to-night as your guest. You are, indeed, the friends that I would have—friends in bad times as well as in good, and we shall see the good times together. I think I will begin by saying a few words to you following on something that I said yesterday in the Albert Hall, because by your very presence here you show your keenness, you show your desire to do something for your party and for the country, and I want to say something, if I can, that may be of help to you in the work that you have to do.

I spoke about the difficulty of a democracy keeping an Empire. Now, democracy is a word often used very loosely, but it is really only a certain form of government, and it is the form of government which exists in our country to-day. I think it is very important for all those who are entering on politics and the study of politics to realise, as I have said before on other occasions, that there is very little difference in space between tyrannies, autocratic governments, popular governments, complete democracies like our own, and governments of licence and anarchy. In other words, you may represent the forms of government which mankind have tried as lying round the circumference of a wheel with tyranny at the top, and working round, as I have described, to anarchy, which inevitably leads back once more to tyranny ; and human governments are always moving imperceptibly in that course. From that fact it has been truly said that the price of liberty is eternal vigilance ; and that is what you have to exercise, to maintain your liberty on the one hand that we may never slip back into tyranny, and to guard that liberty with your lives, if need be, against that licence that leads to anarchy and to unreason, which inevitably, after having destroyed the Empire, would come back to tyranny for its life.

Democracy is the most difficult form of government, and therefore the more worthy of our giving our lives to make it a success. Let us remember that many kings have been ruined by the tongues of well-meaning courtiers. Let our statesmen take care that our people are never ruined by the tongues of able and inspiring friends of democracy. Democracy is no new thing. More than two thousand years ago, in one of the most famous democracies that ever existed, a very great poet, in a play, put these words into the mouth of one of his political characters : " If two orators proposed, one to build ships of war, and the other to increase official salaries, the salaries-man would beat the ships-of-war-man in a canter." Within a generation of the day on which those words were written, that democracy, whose power was based on the sea, perished.

In the British House of Commons there have been found members who have voted, within the last few weeks, both against the construction of new cruisers and in favour of free railway passes. There is nothing new under the sun, and there is nothing that I have ever heard or read of that can be uttered by the extremest of our opponents in any party in their attempt to catch votes that has not already been said in the plays of Aristophanes. Now the instances to which I alluded yesterday as showing incapacity to take a long view, which is so often the great weakness of leaders of a democracy—that incapacity has been shown in the last few days by the decision of the Government in the case of Singapore, and in the case to which Lord Plymouth alluded of certain items of preference with the Dominions. It is a want of imagination and the fear of taking the risk of what could only be a temporary and a local unpopularity, but it is that very cowardice that, in the long run, does so much harm to this form of government. A good motive to my mind can hardly be a sufficient excuse for an act of unwisdom.

Now you here show by your very title that you care sufficiently for your ideals to make sacrifices for them, and to try to induce other people to make sacrifices too. You are not afraid of the word " Empire." I know that there are people who dislike it. They think that it has a militaristic tinge. We may call it a Commonwealth of Nations, a fine title, if we will, but let us remember that the Empire, as we know it, is different from any that has existed hitherto ; for it has not been the creation of conquering armies, although armies have played their part, but our Empire arose from the bone and sinew of our people. It was in the first place commercial adventurers who won our Indian Empire, and how much of our Dominions has not been called into being by men and women who, for reasons of conscience, or desire to find a country in which they could lead a wider, freer life, left our shores voluntarily in a high spirit of adventure ? Thus were the beginnings of our Empire created of our own people and by our own people. And that is why it is our work, and the work of our own people of all classes, to see that that heritage is preserved.

Study these things for yourselves. Learn the history, talk to your friends from the Dominions, and get so lively a sense of what it stands for that you can talk to others about them and teach the real meaning of these great things. Many years ago no task could have seemed more impossible than the creation of a United States ; yet the strength and perseverance of the settlers in that country, and the discoveries subsequently made, enabled them to bring into a United Empire or Commonwealth that great country with its three thousand miles' width of territory and with its varied climates. Some day it may well be that our dream may come true of an Empire whose ways are the great waterways of the world, and in which men shall move for their industry and for their homes from end to end with as little concern as to-day they move from the State of New York to that of California. These ideals have long been among the most cherished ideals of our party. We have attempted to teach the people what we believe would lead to the more speedy fruition of them. We have not yet wholly succeeded, but you have joined yourselves to us although you know that at times we have failed, bringing to us a new enthusiasm of youth and confidence that will carry everything before it.

. . . .

There is only one more subject on which I should like to say a few words, because it is one that I refer to nearly every time I speak, and by this time those who criticise my methods would call them platitudes. Platitudes they may be, but I am going on repeating them until they have some effect. I think it was Sir William Harcourt who said that you had to repeat a thing a dozen times before anyone took any notice. I shall be proud to follow the example of so distinguished a Liberal statesman. I want to speak on one aspect of peace in industry. Now much has been written, and much has been said on that subject. I will only touch on one point. I am convinced, and I am not without experience, that one of the chief things we want is more knowledge and more light—knowledge on the part of each party of the position of the other. Now, to a certain extent, that is not difficult to get. What is difficult to get, and what is of vital importance, is that the men should have knowledge about the industries in which, and for which, they work. What commended to me the miners' agreement was that there you have, in an agreement in one of the greatest trades of the country, that which gives you to a considerable extent what I have always wanted.

Let that example continue and flourish, and let it be modified wherever modifications may be found desirable in practice, but let us see that kind of knowledge made familiar throughout the great industries of the country. The men want to know for their own sakes just these points : something about costs, where the goods they make have to be sold, and in competition with whom they have to be sold, and the conditions under which those goods are produced, where they are produced in competition, and the wages paid. They should also have some knowledge of the amount a business should set aside to meet its repairs and its reserves, and when they have that knowledge they will then know when is the time that they may hope to improve their own condition, they will know then what the imponderables (as they have been called) are, and they can realise, in a way they cannot now, whether or not those who were arguing against them are basing their claims upon facts and are speaking in truth. In other words, it will tend to dissipate that horrible suspicion which causes an atmosphere in which no healthy plant can flourish, and give light and publicity by which alone men can tell whether they are getting a square deal.

Everyone of us here, we hope and believe, by throwing our influence into political life, may do something to better the conditions of our own country. We want to help to better the conditions for our own people. We want to see our people raised, not into a society of State ownership, but into a society in which, increasingly, the individual may become an owner. There is a very famous sentence of Sir Henry Maine's, in which he said that the progress of our civilisation had been of recent centuries a progress on the part of mankind from status to contract. Socialism would bring him back from contract to status.

It is an immense encouragement to me to see a gathering like this—the generosity, the enthusiasm— if we had it through all classes of our party we should be in office for life. You are showing in your youth that you mean to take up the burden, and I say " Good luck to you," for it is the only burden worth taking up. You realise that the State is no cold entity. It is just the sum of all the men and women of our country. If we look at it in that individual way, that it is the men and women of the country we are out to help and to serve, it will lend us enthusiasm. Nothing can help the men and women who compose the State to make the State worthy of this country—nothing can help them more than the kind of service which you are prepared to give— service that will relieve the burden, and service that will make straight the path, never losing in that the sense of the importance of the individual, and the responsibility of each one of us and of all of us to one another and to our Maker.

DISARMAMENT

From a Speech in the House of Commons
23rd July, 1923

VERY little, if anything, has been said to-day about one of the greatest difficulties which we find facing us in dealing with this question, and that is that fighting instinct which is part of human nature. I propose to say a few words about that first, with a view to explaining how, in my view, we have to attempt to eradicate it, or, at least, to combat it, so as to produce that will to peace without which all efforts by legislation, arbitration, rule or otherwise, must be vain. That fighting instinct in man is the instinct of the tiger. It dates from his creation, and was probably given to him to enable him to fight for the survival of his species, for the provision of space in which to bring up his race, and to provide food for it ; and we find through the ages that that instinct, whether in democracy or empire, or among individuals, has had full play. We find it even among men whose political views can be classed as pacifist, and that is the reason why we have often found in history that men of pacifist views were advocating policies which must end, if carried to their logical conclusion, in war.

I need only remind Hon. Members that there was a considerable agitation some little time ago, with which I personally had great sympathy, and which was conducted very largely by those who, in all other respects, were of a peculiarly pacific turn of mind, and that was that this country—if there is any work to be done in this world, it is always our country, and I am thankful for that—that this country should in some way or other rescue Armenia. The only means by which Armenia could have been rescued was at the point of the sword. I may remind Hon. Members that for the thirty years preceding one of the longest and bloodiest struggles in history, the Civil War in America, the anti-slavery agitation in the North-Eastern States was very largely, if not entirely, in the hands of professional pacifists and anti-militarists, and when the agitation had brought matters to the point that it meant either surrendering the principle of anti-slavery or going to war the pacifists, quite rightly in my view, said : " It shall be war," realising, as was said during the late War, that there are times when moral issues may even triumph over peace.

In the same way some of those to-day who are loudest in their protestations of international pacifism are loudest in their protestations that nothing but a class war can save society. No truer word was ever said by a philosopher than was said by Kant, a century ago or more, that we are civilised to the point of wearisomeness, but before we can be moralised we have a long way to go. It is to moralise the world that we all desire, and I have merely mentioned these innate characteristics of human nature to make us realise, as I think we sometimes fail to do, what difficulties there are before us in carrying out a policy with which everyone in this House is in sympathy. We have to remember one more thing besides that, that since the War we must not make the mistake of thinking that what may be war weariness is necessarily an excess of innate good will ; and we cannot help noting that there has arisen in Europe, in the few years since the peace, a strong local feeling in different places of an extreme nationalism which, unless corrected, may bear in what is not of itself an evil thing the seeds of much future peril for the peace and harmony of Europe.

But, taking into full consideration these points, on which I have touched somewhat summarily, I think there are compensations, and I think before I have finished I shall be able to show that the human race is progressing, though slowly, and is full of a conscious, though hardly as yet articulate, desire for further progress in the same direction.

I have often thought, with reference to the late War, that one of the most terrible effects of it— possibly a double effect—has been that it has shown the whole world how thin is the crust of civilisation on which this generation is walking. The realisation of that must have come with an appalling shock to most of us here. But more than that. There is not a man in this House who does not remember the first air raids and the first use of poisoned gas, and the cry that went up from this country. We know how, before the War ended, we were all using both those means of imposing our will upon our enemy. We realise that when men have their backs to the wall they will adopt any means for self-preservation. But there was left behind an uncomfortable feeling in the hearts of millions of men throughout Europe that, whatever had been the result of the War, we had all of us slipped down in our views of what constituted civilisation. We could not help feeling that future wars might provide, with further discoveries in science, a more rapid descent for the human race. There came a feeling, which I know is felt in all quarters of this House, that if our civilisation is to be saved, even at its present level, it behoves all people in all nations to do what they can by joining hands to save what we have, that we may use it as the vantage ground for further progress, rather than run the risk of all of us sliding in the abyss together.

The conscience of the world is not stilled yet, but on the Government side of the House there rests a responsibility which cannot, in the nature of things, be felt by those who sit in opposition. We have to remember that a great deal of what has been said to-day, and if I may use the phrase in all good faith, some of the dreams which have been mentioned to-day are no new thing. We have to remember that in the French wars of Queen Anne's reign there was just the same longing for, and the same dream of, universal peace that so many of us feel to-day. One hundred years ago that same feeling, in different forms, animated many different breasts. Napoleon at St. Helena had dreams too late for him, but dreams of a united Europe with a united congress on the American model, of which he would be the chief and the dictator. At Vienna such dreams were heard of. The Tsar Alexander, a prototype of the late Tsar, whose dreams of peace were shattered only too cruelly, propounded a scheme of Holy Alliance which at that time came to nothing, because he spoke to a world that was not yet ready for it.

We believe that any attempt at this moment to convene an international conference would not only not lead to success, but would lead to the indefinite postponement of any possibility of achieving the ends which we all desire. In my view the moment cannot arise to approach this problem, with any chance of success, until the conditions of Europe with regard to Reparations and the security of frontiers is settled, and I feel that it would be hopeless to expect a definitely favourable answer—to give only two instances ; and I do not wish on this occasion to be more explicit—from France, for instance, before she had obtained a settlement of Reparation and security, or from Poland until she could feel that her frontiers were secure against that gigantic and powerful neighbour along her eastern borders.

The first step to be taken is the step that we are taking now. That is, to attempt a settlement of these existing problems of Reparation, and in taking that step I am animated by as ardent a desire that it may lead ultimately, and at no distant date, to the consideration of these questions which we have been discussing to-day, as I am desirous of it leading to a discussion and settlement of those questions which have kept the countries of Europe apart during all the years which have succeeded the Great War. Let us never forget that sometimes in the darkest day the beginnings of better things are not only attempted but successfully achieved. It was in the darkest days of the struggle of the Thirty Years' War that Grotius worked on international law and led to the foundation of that science which, though it has not brought peace to the world, has yet brought into being a code which has helped the world in its peaceful development, and will continue to do so.

It has been during those dark days of the last three or four years that the Washington Conference was held, which has led to a limitation of naval armaments that, until that Conference was held, I am convinced the statesmen of all countries would have considered to have been impossible, impossible even to have been debated, and impossible in its fulfilment. This year, some of the most valuable exploratory work has been done, and is being done, by the League of Nations. The League of Nations has been occupied in considering this very question of disarmament, and the possibility of linking it up with guarantees of security, universal in their application as such guarantees must be : and such a universality is, indeed, a first and absolute essential to make any prospect hopeful of limitation of armaments.

Now, those efforts of the League of Nations are on the point of taking concrete form in the shape of proposed Treaties, which will be submitted to the Governments of Europe for their consideration, probably after the meeting in September of the General Assembly of the League of Nations. I can promise, at least for this Government, and I am certain that the same will be true of all the leading Governments of Europe, that the work that the League of Nations has done, the form in which their work will be presented, will be examined, not only with the sympathy and the interest that such work deserves, but with an earnest desire, at the first moment when it appears to be practicable, that the aims of the League, if not in the exact form in which they have suggested they should be brought about, shall be brought into effect in Europe.

As was well said by the Hon. Member for Preston (Mr. T. Shaw), in the course of his speech, there is one great instrument of peace in this world, and that is the British Empire. It is a great instrument, not only in its size, and its population, and its wealth, but more than ever a great instrument in this, that it is not only an Empire, but it is a large assembly of free nations, not all of the same kin or the same tongue, but animated largely by a common purpose, and all alike equally desirous of seeing extended in every corner of that Empire or Commonwealth those ideas of liberty, and justice, and freedom which we believe are in our hearts, and which we hope to see spread throughout our Empire and throughout the world. In that collection of nations, which now spreads throughout the world, there is something of hope for the human race, because though it may seem a dream, it may yet some day be possible for peoples in so distracted a Continent as Europe to feel there may be something for them to learn from the development, from the union, and from the ideals of our great Empire, and we may possibly be able to show them a better way, which in years to come they may tread, and find the solution that to-day seems so difficult.

As I have tried to explain to the House we cannot see our way to accept this Motion and take immediate steps, believing as we do that such steps would be rather a bar to future progress than a help. Yet I do say this, that when we are sufficiently fortunate, as I pray we may be, to have seen brought about, with our aid, such a settlement in European conditions as I indicated earlier on, then the time will be ripe and we shall be ready to take our part, in so far as we can, whether through such schemes as have been proposed already or through others, in bringing about that limitation of armaments which we believe to be essential for the future progress of civilised mankind. It is an easy thing to say, as many men say to-day, that this country should cut herself adrift from Europe, but we must remember that our island story is told, and that with the advent of the aeroplane we ceased to be an island. Whether we like it or not, we are indissolubly bound to Europe, and we shall have to use, and continue to use, our best endeavours to bring to that Continent that peace in which we and millions of men up and down Europe have an equal belief and an equal faith.

MISCELLANEOUS

SCOTLAND

St. Andrew's Day Festival of the Royal Scottish Corporation

30th November, 1925

It is a great honour for one who is not hundred per cent. a Scot to preside over the anniversary of the Corporation. The Charity goes back even further than 261 years. It goes back to the time when the throne was transferred from Edinburgh to London, and in the wake of that throne began the migration southwards which, in after years, attained such great proportions. It being a Scottish army, the casualties by the way were few, but it is a great tribute to the race that from the beginning they made preparations to deal with those casualties. Attempts were made to succour the fallen, attempts which have gained in force from generation to generation as the need becomes greater, so that, as the years go by, there is hardly a family which has attained prosperity in London whose name may not be found in the annals of the Corporation as having helped to make provision for their less fortunate brothers and sisters. In the face of a patriotism so insistent and so persistent it is not necessary for me this night to beg for this great organisation. You have responded to its call already with your traditional and your national generosity.

Now, I would like, as an Englishman, not without connection with a certain part of Scotland, to offer a few observations on the virtues of the Scot and on the impression that the Scot has made in England ; and I think perhaps, speaking as an Englishman, that there is one thing above all others which we owe to you, and one thing in which the Scot has set an example, which we would do well to imitate. There is nothing that fills me with more admiration than the way in which your people for generations have held up that standard of plain living and high thinking—a lesson which to-day a world that would, if it could, be a world of high living and plain thinking, needs more than ever before. Nothing has made Scotland what she is more than the magnificent system of parochial education, which she had years before any other part of the British Isles. The picture of the Scottish student with his sack of oatmeal, leaving his work for part of the year, living and drawing on the frugality and self-sacrifice of father and mother, brother and sister, in the pursuit and attainment of knowledge for the sake of knowledge, is an example to the whole world, and what your Scots have to be mindful of is that in this age, when education is tending to become spoon-fed, you do not allow yourselves to lose sight of the ideals of the past generations.

When I think of all the lessons you have to give us, I am always struck by the fact that of Scotsmen, I think, perhaps alone, the English people are in no way either jealous or envious. Whatever be the reason, the English have always taken the Scots to their hearts as blood brothers. I do not think it is difficult to give the reason, and I think the reason may be traced to one man of genius. For a long time after the Union it would seem that the Union itself afforded no stimulus—whatever else it may have done—to Scottish literature. One of your own most famous writers in the last century said that at that time you had " theologic ink and Jacobite blood, with gall enough in both cases to have blotted out the intellect of the country "—and when David Hume and Adam Smith came they were still drawing from France rather than from their own soil. But a few years later, by the grace of God, you threw up two men of genius, Walter Scott and Robert Burns. You had, as no other nation ever has had, a man of yourselves to interpret you to the neighbouring kingdom—that was Walter Scott ; for however ardent an admirer of Burns you may be, no one could call Burns an interpreter to Englishmen. Scott did a great deal for your country. There was, of course, patriotism before Scott appeared, but he deepened, enriched and ennobled it in a thousand ways for the Scots themselves. All that honours the ancestry of the Scot and the kindred of the Scot, the virtues and the noble deeds of your ancestors, the heroism of the common people—all that he gave you, and through that many in his generation, and in the generation that came after, have felt more than they had ever felt before that they had a country to live for, an ancestry to live up to. It was a tremendous stimulus.

But the greatest service he rendered was the interpretation of Scotland to England. Take myself as a typical Englishman. By the time I was ten I had read the *Tales of a Grandfather*, and had read all his poems and half his novels. Since then, I suppose, not a year goes by that I do not read some of them again, and whenever I go to Edinburgh I go down to Castle Street and look at the bay window where he stood and the door where he welcomed Pet Marjorie. He said when he first wrote that he wished to do for Scotland what Maria Edgeworth did for Ireland ; but how many people of to-day outside those who love books—which is not the same thing as borrowing from Mudie's—ever read Maria Edgeworth ? Had there been a Walter Scott for Ireland there would have been no Boundary Commission sitting to-day, and I should have been able to have devoted my week-end, as I had intended, to preparing a speech worthy of this occasion.

That is not all that Walter Scott did. How impossible it would have seemed to Boswell and

Dr. Johnson, when they travelled in the Hebrides, if anyone had told them that within sixty years there would arise a genius who would bring the English King to Edinburgh and put him in a kilt, that a genius would arise under the spell of whose wand the Lowlander would adopt the garb of the robbers of the North. I remember when I was in Scotland this autumn I was asked humorously why I did not wear a kilt when in Scotland. I said the last time my ancestors wore a kilt was at Culloden, and I leave it for the English to wear it when they go to Scotland. If it had not been for Walter Scott you would never have seen the kilt south of the Grampians, and the result is that we English—a prosaic race—cannot look at Scotland or at a Scot except through those glasses tinted with romance and history, those glasses that Walter Scott made us wear ; and, while we are looking at you with the vision of the Wizard of the North, wrapped in admiration, you attend strictly to business ! When Scott wrote his first novel the " Forty-five " was only sixty years back. It seems long years away from us. The Industrial Revolution, which Scott hardly understood, has almost submerged us.

" The successor of Monkbarns does not exchange ideas with the successor of Edie Ochiltree. He meets his fellow lairds in a London club. Edie Ochiltree has left the bonny burnsides for the city slums ; Mrs. Mucklebackit sells her ware to a London fishmonger ; and Captain M'Intyre hires his moor to a wealthy American ; while

Mr. Blattergowl is not the unique minister of a unique parish."

And yet, though there is an element of truth in these things, there remains in you that indestructible love of your own people and your own soil ; and, in my view at least, it is largely for this reason that you, in spite of a certain amount of industrialising of your country, have not yet been submerged by industrialism to the extent that a large part of the southern portion of Great Britain has been. So long as you keep your contact with nature, so long as the Highlands are left, so long as your great agricultural country is left, those roots are left in the soil which alone can propagate that plant of tradition which means so much to you, as it does to the countryman in England.

If you ask an Englishman what he thinks of Scotland in contradistinction to what comes in his mind when he thinks of England, we think of the heather and the moors, and we see your northern country as we should see it in June, ablaze with the glory of the broom. Those are the pictures that rise in our minds, and if I were asked what represents the soul of Scotland I could not answer better than by the reply which was given many years ago to a relative of mine in New Zealand by an old Scottish farmer. My relative asked him how long the traditions that your people bring from home last in a new country, and the old settler replied, " The porridge and the heather and the Psalms of David last to the third generation as a sustenance for body and spirit." And may they abide for ever, because —and I speak as an Englishman—were the Scot to pass, with his history, with his tradition, with his character, there would pass at the same time from earth a large part of the heroism and the romance of the world, those intangible qualities which, perhaps more than anything else, make us capable of plain living, high thinking and great deeds.

IRELAND

St. Patrick's Day Banquet
17th March, 1926

No man can stand here to-night before an audience like this, occupying the position which I do, without asking himself what has happened that such a gathering, that such a company, is possible in London to-night. I feel, perhaps, it means that the secular struggle is drawing—has drawn—to a close ; it means that you recognise too generously the little that I have been able to do with my colleagues to help Ireland over a stile.

Having safely surmounted the stile, two facts stand out before the statesmen of Ireland and the statesmen of England. It is not for me in my position to speak, as Mr. MacVeagh did, with the yearning of the Irish for an Ireland one and indivisible, but I still say this, that the fact that by that recent settlement it was recognised in Ireland that there was a problem in the North has, for the first time, rendered the solution at some time possible, because as the Minister for Justice of the Free State said, it is a problem not perhaps soluble at the present time, but one that possibly only time can solve. To solve any problem the first essential is the recognition of it.

Secondly, Ireland is governed to-day from Merrion Street, not from Dublin Castle or from Whitehall. That, I believe, marks the close, as I said, of a secular conflict; but before we glance at the future, in the few words I have to say to you to-night, I do not think we shall waste our time in dwelling for a few minutes on the paths that we have trodden in the past, and the paths we are treading to-day.

We have been too used through the generations and the centuries to conflict between our peoples and our nations, and we know—now that we can look at these things from afar, I trust—that the root of that conflict went deep down into the characters of the two peoples, and that those characters themselves were moulded by their very different histories. In Ireland you look back, as the Celt always will look back, to the golden age. You were nourished on memories of that time when Ireland was, according to the tradition of her historians and of folk-lore, the island of saint and scholar. You look back to the work of St. Patrick, who, I may remark, first converted Ulster before he took in hand the rest of Ireland. We have relics of those days in the luminous pages of your manuscripts and in the rare work of cross and chalice which now lie in your museums. All that time, while we in England were growing slowly into a united nation, with a consolidated government, in Ireland, whatever the reason, the great privilege was not yours because for centuries there was disunion, and the stable government which broadened from age to age, following precedent with us, had no such chance with you. This struggle for centuries culminated at a time when hell was let loose throughout the whole of Europe, and it is good that we should now forget those days. With you, as with the rest of Europe—to use the words of one of your own historians—" The soul of man was bloodied and bruised," but now murdering hate is a dead thing, and once more in this struggling world the love of God has some chance to contend against the eternal stupidity of mankind.

The rule of reason is slowly emerging from the riot of violence, and is throughout the world cleansing the foul parts of the infected world with its medicine. In that process the veil of illusion has been rent, but as compensation the rhetoricians are silent, and it always seems to me that, with the first sense of responsibility and the passage into full freedom, one of the most difficult times that can face the Celt confronts you. For the Celt of all nations is a man who has dwelt with his dreams, and to be plunged from his dreams into the white light of the twentieth century is indeed a staggering shock, and in that fierce light it is little wonder if with many another man he finds himself precipitated from the heights on which he fancied he dwelt into a pit of depression and of cynicism. But all these things will pass.

They are but the consequent evils of the day, and the people will learn that salvation comes to them by the industry of their own hands and by the work of their own brains.

If they cannot achieve it in that way, they will be no more able to achieve it from Merrion Street than from Whitehall. The people must save themselves. It is a hard and painful task, as we all know, to build up. It is easy enough to destroy. It is easier to face death for an ideal than it is to face the daily duty and the daily drudgery against the forces of vice and ignorance, which have to be faced in the attainment of any ideal. But Ireland is fortunate in this, that in the North she has a statesman, an Irishman and a man of deep wisdom ; and in Dublin, in the Free State, you have as statesmen men who have looked into the eyes of both life and death. They are facing an almost insuperable burden to-day with courage and honesty rare amongst statesmen.

We in England wish them well with all our hearts. We want the two Governments of Ireland to have fair play from the world. We want them to have a fair chance of settling down to their work, and so far as we are concerned I think we have given proof of the sincerity of our desires for the prosperity of Ireland. I have only one word more to add. I have been told that just as the virtue of truth, on which perhaps we English are apt to credit ourselves, is sometimes presented in a form not dissimilar from aggressiveness and insolence—I have been told that by those who do not love us—so I have been told that the Celtic virtue of courtesy is sometimes extended to a point where it almost becomes insincerity. As an illustration, I have been told that if you ask an Irish peasant how far you are from your destination, he is always more anxious to give you satisfaction than information, and the illimitable distance you have to travel before you reach your journey's end—the land of heart's desire—is to him only " just beyond the hill." That is a failing of all people with prophetic souls.

That ideal state, to which Mr. Cosgrave would lead his people along an Irish road, and to which I would lead mine along an English road, we tell each other is just over the hills. We know in our hearts we shall never reach it, but if we did not believe that it was only just over the hills we should never have the strength to go through that dreary, dusty walk in attending to the needs of the caravan on its journey day by day throughout this world. Our courses are set the same. Our goal is the same. Our method of travelling may be different, but it is because our paths run alongside, and because you have asked me here to-night, that I feel we may now fairly join hands as we proceed across that narrow strip of water, those of us who live on this side and you who live on that.

WALES

I SUPPOSE that when an Englishman comes to dine with you he tries to find some link by which he may explain his presence. In asking me you have asked one that was born and bred, and whose people have lived for a very long time, in those border counties where in the old days we knew a great deal about you. In Shropshire, whence my family migrated into Worcestershire to get a little farther from the border, there are still to-day, I believe, about one-fifth of all the castles that exist in England. Why they were crowded into that narrow area I have no idea. And when I do go home and look from my garden, four miles across the valley is the hill on which, according to tradition, Owen Glendower had his camp, on, I think, the last invasion of our county by the Welsh.

My family has some connection with Wales if you go back far enough. Long, long years ago there were two Baldwins who tossed a coin at some remote place on the Continent, and one went East, where he became King of Jerusalem, and thereby preceded by about a thousand years Sir Herbert Samuel, and

249

another went West, crossed over, first into England and then into Wales, where his name was softened, as you soften everything in Wales, and he gave his name to what we in England call the county of Montgomery.

Another century slipped by, and an archbishop of my name, translated to Canterbury from Worcester, went on a pilgrimage into Wales. He went with a very specific object. He knew that the Welsh were devout, and he had been told that they made most admirable foot soldiers, so he tried to secure them for the Crusades, and he took with him an eloquent archdeacon and journalist by name Giraldus. I regret to say, however pure one's motives, the twelfth century differed little from the present. There were those who said that my ancestor, if I may call him so, really went to Wales because he wished by celebrating Mass at the High Altar of each of the four Welsh cathedrals to establish the supremacy of Canterbury. I don't know whether that was true, but some of the priests in Wales, thinking that it was, did their best to impede his progress, though without success, and the only part of Wales in which this holy man met with an unfavourable reception, I regret to say, was in the county of Carnarvon. It is a source of infinite regret to me that the distinguished representative of that part of Wales [1] is unable to be present to-night, for we might then have got to the bottom of this secular trouble. But so undisturbed am I by what happened all those centuries ago that I am thinking this summer of starting on a pilgrimage myself, not by

[1] Mr. Lloyd George.

palfrey, but by motor-car, and I shall leave Bewdley by what we still call the Welsh Gate and go to preside over—a word of ten letters signifying a national festival—to be held at a little town of eight letters.[1]

It is strange, indeed, to look at the border country to-day and to think that it was for so long by Severn and Wye a scene of interminable raids. Now there is no more peaceful part of England than that of which the Shropshire poet wrote :

> In valleys of springs of rivers,
>   By Ony and Teme and Clun,
> A country of pleasant livers,
>   The quietest under the sun.

We tried, it is true, in those days to keep you out of England, and now we come to do homage to you in our own capital, of which you have almost taken possession. Not for the first time in history have the Greeks defeated their conquerors, and, indeed, this country had a very narrow escape in the years immediately succeeding the War from the imposing of Welsh as the diplomatic language of Europe.

There are times in the life of a Prime Minister when he is able, not without difficulty, to get away from his arduous work and disappear for a short time unseen by the public and unknown to the Press. I had the good fortune so to disappear and find myself by accident in the studio of a Chelsea sculptor. When there I saw an exquisitely beautiful statue of a young shepherd, the original of the figure which now stands in a mountain village in Merioneth-shire—the figure of a poet (Hedd Wyn) who took his

[1] Pwllheli.

part in the Great War. You have all heard of the story of this private soldier in the trenches who had written a poem for your great festival at Birkenhead, and how he was killed on Pilkem Ridge before he received the crown that would have been given to him ; and the sculptor explained to me that the poet's Hero had been composed of Prometheus and the Man of Nazareth—the energy that makes for kindliness and beauty ; whenever I think of Wales, it is not of her industrial areas, but of the country, and I look upon that figure as a type of what our rural civilisation can produce. That poet has again proved the truth of the old saying that " The Celt goes forth to battle and has always fallen " ; but there is the additional truth that there are some defeats which mean more than victories, and which are in themselves victories everlasting.

Finally, I would like to remind you of the beautiful words used by St. David the last time he spoke to his own people :

"Be joyful and keep your faith, and believe and perform the small things which you have heard and seen with me, and I will go the road which our fathers have travelled. Be courageous while you are upon the earth, for you will not see me any more in this world."

If that can still be a message to the people of these islands, and if they will listen to it, we shall have nothing to fear in the future, and the name of St. David will go down the ages blessed by the English as well as by the Welsh.

GLASGOW

At Glasgow

1st October, 1925

IT is a matter of peculiar pride to become a burgess of a city which is one of the most famous in the world. There can be few corners of the world into which the fame and name of Glasgow have not penetrated, and where there cannot be found some product of your manifold energies, and, in these latter days, where the echoes of the voices of your Parliamentary representatives have not been heard. I know full well that the honour you have done me is to me as first Minister of the Crown, and I believe you have made me this presentation as a recognition that I have tried, at any rate, to discharge my duties as the chief servant of the people in no party spirit, and that you mean it as an encouragement to try to go forward and do better.

I am receiving the great honour from you at a time of very grave difficulty. No progressive country has ever been free or ever will be free from difficulties. We have come through a prolonged and terrific struggle for our very existence, we are borne down under a burden of taxation resulting from that struggle, we are perplexed by the changes occurring under our eyes in the channels of the world trade on which we are so dependent, and we are profoundly depressed at the thought of the numbers of unemployed, and of the continuance of unemployment.

Nothing could be easier than to paint a sombre picture full of shadows, and to ask ourselves : " Does Scotland stand where she did ? " or " Is England played out ? " But that would not be a true picture. The life of Glasgow is the story in miniature of the whole country—the gradual evolution, the increase in population, power and prosperity. It was not so long ago, as the generations of men are reckoned, that Glasgow was but a village, and almost before the people realised what was happening her traders began to go out over the seas of the world. The Clyde was deepened, coal and iron were discovered in your neighbourhood, your great series of pioneers and inventors from James Watt to Lord Kelvin made their names and the name of the city known throughout the world, and in two short centuries Glasgow passed from being a little country town into a mighty city of a million souls, which has drawn into its vortex not only the people from the glens of the North, but from the farming country and, indeed, from overseas, so that you now have a fourth part of the population of Scotland packed together in this area in a density greater than that which exists in most of our English towns. The story of Glasgow

is thus a story of stupendous adventure and achievement, answering to some of the deepest instincts of
human nature. Such a story has not been achieved
without strain and conflict, and even loss. Past
generations have left to us a city, and we have to
maintain its character, noted particularly for the
fierce energy of its people, the high quality of their
workmanship, and the boldness of their municipal
enterprise. It is true to say that the labours of
Glasgow, industrial, commercial and municipal, have
profoundly affected the current of modern civilisation in all parts of the world, and have affected it
largely for good.

This has been done by the co-operation of mind
and brain. There has been no standing still ; there
is no standing still to-day. We have to remember
that while in the time of our fathers the changes that
always came, came slowly, what is apt to disconcert
us is the speed at which changes come to-day—
changes social, industrial and commercial. To-day
the chemist is revolutionising industry. We are
beginning to make various things by artificial processes which might have seemed like miracles a
quarter of a century ago. To-day I am to have the
pleasure of seeing a great municipal experiment
which you are making in order to learn whether you
cannot light your city, dye your clothes, clear your
atmosphere and drive your motor cars out of coal.
It is this ceaseless activity that has made Glasgow
what she is, and that is the hope of her future.

What Burke said of the State is true of the city. We have a partnership, not only between those who are living, but a partnership over many generations with those who have gone before us and with those who will follow us. The life of a city is a continuous thing, a living organisation, and its citizens are members not only of one another but heirs of those who went before. And so, while we inherit a civilised way of life and opportunities and comforts and pleasures far beyond the dreams of our ancestors, it is also true that we cannot escape inheriting the very texture of city life, the results of the failings of good men and of the sins of evil men.

No problem which faces Glasgow is greater than that of housing, our inheritance from an age when the Industrial Revolution swept so quickly through the land that it had done its work before people realised that it had come at all. Quite apart from the essential wrong of such conditions of housing as still exist to-day, there is no doubt that those conditions are the most fertile source of that social discontent which is known so well in this city, as in other congested parts of the kingdom. Grievous as it may be to see social discontent, it is yet a better thing than cynical indifference or lazy acquiescence in conditions such as I saw in this city yesterday afternoon. I know how aggravated the problem is here, particularly through the tenement-house system and through the rush of immigration. It is not for us to apportion blame ; it is a waste of time to do so. We are all to blame, and we have all come short of perfection. Let us see that our sympathy is not wasted in noisy declamation or in mere fault-finding. Let us rather wed the social enthusiasm that does exist here to experience and reason. The task of improving the worst quarters in our great cities is hard enough to demand the co-operation of the best men and women of all classes, and those who withstand such an aim, whether from a selfish regard for their wealth or property, or from a desire to monopolise their skill and exploit the city—these people, in whatever ranks of life they are found, are the worst enemies of the communal life.

I am convinced myself that the day will come when we shall have to eviscerate our great cities, a tremendous task, but one to which the imagination and the vision and the wisdom of the best of us may well be devoted. The task is enormous, and therefore it is all the better worth doing. I like to think that even at a time like this, when we are preoccupied with unemployment and the hardship arising out of it, we are yet giving our minds to try to raise up in this kingdom better, healthier, more beautiful communities than exist to-day, and I should like to think that I am becoming a burgess of your city at a time when the public conscience is stirred on these matters as never before, and when in Glasgow there are those who are striving might and main to make Glasgow what she once was and might be again, namely, one of the fairest cities in the kingdom.

In that high task I would fain be associated with my fellow-burgesses. I shall follow you in your struggle to solve the problems that surround you, knowing that as you accomplish them you are not only making Glasgow better, happier, healthier and more prosperous, but are contributing in large measure to the security, prosperity and happiness of the people at large in these islands which are our home.

ANGLO-AMERICAN FRIENDSHIP

THE ANNUAL RE-UNION DINNER OF THE BRITISH WAR MISSIONS TO THE UNITED STATES

29*th April*, 1925

LOOKING back, I think that if there was one thing that struck our delegates, on whatever task they were engaged in America, it was the amazing and the generous hospitality showered on all alike by their new friends in every part of the United States. Apart from the personal side they were struck by the immense effort that the United States made in those early days of the war, when they showed an example of enthusiasm, of hard work, and of receptiveness to ideas—when they showed that natural characteristic of hero-worship, and came forward to do everything in their power to help their Allies to bring to a successful issue the terrible undertaking in which they were engaged.

Living as I was at that time in London, and working at the Treasury, I cannot help in a gathering of this kind recalling the day when the first American troops appeared in London. I do not know how the reception of those troops affected the Americans themselves. The outlook was different to them from what it was to us, but I shall never forget standing on the Horse Guards Parade watching them marching by, not to a storm of cheers, which perhaps some had expected, but in a deep, profound silence, which to me was far more moving than any cheers.

Speaking for myself, I understand what was passing through the minds and hearts of that crowd. As we looked at these young men, the pick of their nation, so fresh, so keen, so enthusiastic, with their fine military bearing, the thought that was prominent in my mind was how they had come three thousand, four thousand and five thousand miles to Europe to help us.

I wondered how it looked to them. I thought of the homes from which they had come, the strangeness of the surroundings to them, their feeling of fresh enthusiasm, of our feeling of worn but grim determination begotten of the three years of hell through which we had passed, and I could not help thinking how little, in the triumph of that march, they could realise what that fiery furnace was towards which they were going, and from which few of those early regiments could ever hope to return. It seemed to me then as impossible to cheer as I always find it impossible to applaud when I have heard the most beautiful music that stirs the soul rather than the head.

But, after all, we are here to-night to celebrate friendships which were made in a time such as I have endeavoured to depict, friendships which certainly individually, I believe, in hundreds of cases have only grown stronger with the passage of time. We thought then much of our combined and united influence on the world. Possibly the freshness of that feeling, maybe in both countries, has to some extent evaporated in the strenuous years of peace which have followed. But there is just as much need, if not more need, to-day for that understanding, for that co-operation, and for that mutual help, as ever there was in the time of war. Strangers as many of us were to each other, we rapidly became acquaintances, and acquaintances became friends, and gatherings such as these will keep those friendships alive, if indeed anything be necessary for that purpose, and we hope that through us they may help to keep alive the friendship of the nations.

If I may say one more word to the English here—it is not necessary to you, but it is necessary to our country people, and I look to you to teach our country people—it is this : it is quite true that we and the Americans have much in common, but what most English people who do not know America forget is that the essential thing for mutual understanding is to realise what we have not got in common.

The root of any differences which may occur at any time between our two peoples is the root of most of the trouble in this world—it is the root of ignorance. And it is because it is one of the objects of this society to dispel and eradicate that ignorance that I rejoice in its existence and in its continuance. I think probably many of you taught America something of the nature, the quality, and the character of our people, just as many of those who came from America during the war taught the same lesson to our people. But it rests with you, and I am glad to hear it from Sir Thomas Royden to-night, to carry out the good work and to teach those who have not had our advantages what we ourselves have learned, because friendship at the best of times is fragile ; a friendship will not run long of itself ; friendship requires care and consideration.

I do not think there is much more on that subject I can say to you, and I think that what I would say has been far better expressed by others than I could express it myself. I will content myself by using some words which were uttered more than sixty years ago, which epitomise all that I would say, and all that I hope, and all that I believe :

" Whatever else may happen, whatever misfortune may befall your country or my own, the peace and friendship which now exist between the two nations will be, as it shall be my desire to make them, perpetual."

These were the words of Abraham Lincoln. Since those words were uttered we have passed through Armageddon together. May the friendship between the two nations, based on mutual knowledge and understanding, be perpetual for the benefit of the whole world.

FRIENDLY SOCIETIES

AT STOURPORT, AT THE ANNIVERSARY DINNER OF THE ANCIENT ORDER OF FORESTERS (STOUR VALLEY)

18th February, 1924

IT is not wasting words to try to realise what the great friendly society movement stands for. Like many other good things, it is of pure English growth, and owes its origin to the common people from whom many of the best things have come. It springs, as it were, from the soil, and has been a great instrument during a period of rapid change in instructing our people in some of the greatest of the principles which should guide their lives, as well as in branches of work and learning in many subjects in which they could have no other teacher.

Immersed as my life has become in political work, I am glad that in the friendly society movement we know no politics. Politics have such powers of penetrating most things that I am thankful that this movement has never been captured by any of the political machines, and I hope its leaders will see to it in the future that it remains a thing apart.

A man entering a court or lodge gets his first

insight into the common problem of Government ; learns to control himself by working with others ; learns to work with others for the benefit of others, and to exercise discrimination and judgment. I have also seen how the savings of the many can be utilised to fertilise the public services and the social activities of the country. The whole spirit of the movement is service for others, a spirit which is more wanted in England and in every country of the world to-day than any other ; but because of the great influence and position of our own country there is no other in which that spirit needs to be more manifested, since the greater part of mankind looks to us as to the one country which they hope and believe will set the example to the world in the stability and probity of its finances and in its willingness to be of service to the rest of the distracted world. By teaching our own people the spirit of service which the friendly societies inculcate, we are playing our part in making our democracy fitter and nobler, and by doing that we are not only helping ourselves but the whole world.

HARROW

THANKS be to Heaven there is in every English boy an unconscious but impregnable resistance to every form of pressure made by any schoolmaster who works him too hard or tries to put too much inside him. I know that was so in my own case and in that of many who have done far more work in the world than I have. It is to this that Englishmen owe so largely the careful cultivation of their physical growth. They let the body grow, undisturbed by mental storms, until they got into their early twenties, and then they go out into the world able to graft the sane mind on to the sane body. They have not worked out their minds before they come to tackle the problems of the world.

I cannot help going back into the past, seeing so many faces which call up memories of forty years ago. When a small boy at a private school I was taken, wearing a new top hat and an Eton jacket, to Lords, where I watched the Harrow Eleven winning a great victory. I remember that at the tail of the team there walked from the pavilion by far the largest schoolboy I had ever seen. The first ball that boy got he put well into the old pavilion. The boy's name was Ronald M'Neill.

I can single out to-night a man, whom I remember as captain of my house football eleven, who has just returned after a most distinguished period of service in Persia and Mesopotamia. He is known to the whole Empire as Sir Percy Cox. Not far from him is another whose name I hardly dare mention, because in those distant years he was my fag. He combined immaculate cleanliness with an immaculate manner. I am proud to call him my Right Honourable learned and gallant friend Jack Seely. Sprinkled here and there throughout the room, some of them disguised in clerical dress, are a lot of distinguished men whom I remember as ruffians in the football field.

There is no feeling that remains longer in life than the feeling that one has at thirteen or fourteen years of age, and I assure the Captain of the Eleven here to-night that in the breasts of all the small boys at Harrow to-day, that feeling of awe and reverence with which he is personally regarded will be as vivid in their bosoms fifty years hence as it is to-day.

I must pay tribute to the Fourth Form Room. The first time I made its acquaintance was when I sat for an entrance examination, and I remember so well my disappointment at finding I was among the rejected. I got over it, however, in subsequent years, when I learnt that two of the most distinguished men in public life to-day had shared my fate : one is the First Lord of the Admiralty, and the other—it is the first time I have ever been classed with first-class brains—no less a person than the late Lord Chancellor, the Earl of Birkenhead. Happy the school whose outcasts and rejected can yet make good in after life !

When the call came to me to form a Government, one of my first thoughts was that it should be a Government of which Harrow should not be ashamed. I remembered how in previous Governments there had been four or, perhaps, five Harrovians, and I determined to have six. To make a Cabinet is like making a jig-saw puzzle fit, and I managed to make my six fit by keeping the post of Chancellor of the Exchequer for myself. I think we have good reason to be content. I am very proud that it has fallen to my lot to be the next Prime Minister after Palmerston to come from Harrow, and it is a special source of pride and joy to me to know that Mr. Yates Thompson is here to-night, for he was the Head of the School when Palmerston was Prime Minister. I hope with all my heart that the present Head of the School may live to be as old as Mr. Yates Thompson, be as much respected, and be able to look back with as much pleasure at the share he took in our gathering this evening.

I have known no occasion on which it has been more difficult to find the right word to express my feelings. I stand here to-night among men who have made good in this world for their own sakes and for the sake of the School in every walk of life. I think they will agree with me—stern self-critics as all men must be who have made good—that there is only one form of congratulation in this world that is worth anything, and that is the expression of good will and the expression from your own peers—that is, from the men who themselves are working in the hard places of the world and trying to make those rough places smooth—that you have tried to do your duty. I realise as well as anyone here that the kindness you have shown me and the welcome you have given me are not so much a tribute to achievement—that, please God! may come later—but as holding out the hand to one from the same School who is now taking on himself the heaviest burden in the world. You mean by your greeting to assure me that you wish me well, as I know you do, and that whether I succeed or fail you have the belief in me that as a son of the Hill I will run straight ; that I will bear my share of the burden ; that if I fail I will not whine ; and that if success is mine I shall not be puffed up ; but that I will try in all things to follow in the footsteps of those who have trodden this same difficult path before me ; and that I will, with God's help, do nothing in the course of an arduous and a difficult career which shall cause any Harrovian to say of me that I have failed to do my best to live up to the highest ideals of the School.

SOME ANCESTORS

FROM A SPEECH TO THE NONCONFORMIST
UNIONIST LEAGUE

8th *April*, 1924

I OWE a great deal of my public and private life to my Nonconformist ancestry. It is curiously crossed with two very strong strains which work sometimes comfortably and sometimes very uncomfortably side by side. I have a Quaker strain that goes back to the earliest days of the Quakers, when one of my ancestors went out in the reign of William III. as a missionary to the American Colonies. He devoted half a century mainly to missionary work there and in the West Indies, where ultimately he died, leaving a name which was perhaps the most prominent and the best known of the Quaker missionaries in those Colonies.

This Quaker blood is peculiarly persistent, and I attribute to it a certain obstinacy which I find co-existing with one of the most placable dispositions that ever a man had. I find sometimes that when I conceive a matter to be one of principle I feel I would rather go to the stake than give way. It

sometimes brings me into trouble, and has brought
my friends into trouble, but I am afraid that characteristic will remain with me as long as I live.

But all these things have their compensations.
The Quakers were by far the most persecuted body
of the Nonconformists, and that strain of Quakerism
makes one absolutely impervious to the abuse which
necessarily occurs in public life.

To come to more modern times, I have a rather
remarkable record—no less than half my great-
grandfathers were Presidents of Conference. I am
immensely proud of this ancestry, because they set
an example which it is not easy to live up to, and
up to which, in the earlier part of my life, I failed
signally to live. I quoted the instance while I was
in Scotland of one of my great-grandfathers who
was the son of a man who fled from Scotland after
the " Forty-five." He was a personal follower of
John Wesley, and was, if I remember aright, ordained
by him to the Wesleyan ministry. He was a man
who never could have had more than a couple of
pounds a week, but he was a natural scholar. He
taught himself many languages, and, more remarkable still, he educated his own eldest son to take a
scholarship at Cambridge, and in the next generation
the same performance was repeated by the gaining
of a scholarship at Oxford by the son of a father
who must have been brought up on something
very like that narrow and meagre income. It was,
indeed, a time of plain living and high thinking.

If there is one thing more than another of which I feel ashamed to-day, it is to think how I, with the chances I had in youth—and I venture to think with the capacity to take equal advantage of them— wasted so much time when I was at the University and failed to follow in the footsteps of those who had gone before me, with far less advantages. But these things come home to us as we get older. I think, as years go by, we look more and more to those who have gone before us, and we want to feel that when our time comes to pass away we may leave some record behind us to make those who follow less ashamed of us.

A WAR MEMORIAL

At the Unveiling of the Board of Trade War Memorial

19th December, 1923

THERE is no greater honour that can fall to a man than to be asked to unveil a memorial of this kind. I am grateful to those who asked me to perform this ceremony to-day. All over the land, in stone and bronze, have arisen these memorials ; memorials to help us in our recollections and to tell the world and the unborn generations of the magnitude of the sacrifice by which we attained our victory. And the unborn generations in some way are happier than we, for to them will be revealed in their true perspective the magnitude and the issues of the contest, and from them will be hidden some of the controversies, the sordid things, the selfishness and the greed which arose among the good deeds like poisonous fungi, the recollection of which will pass away with our generation. But even now, those who are here can see and estimate what the endurance and the courage of our own people were during those years, and it should be an inspiration to us for the rest of our lives.

There never was a war before this, at any rate for our country, in which the whole people was engaged directly or indirectly ; a war in which men went forth to fight in the full consciousness of what they did. Not a man, whose name is commemorated on this tablet, but went forth with the full knowledge that he was fighting for what he and his countrymen believed to be right, for the liberties of the world, and those who fell, fell in a belief, perhaps hardly uttered by themselves, that somehow or another their lives might be given to promote the betterment of this world.

Seven millions perished in Europe, and here we commemorate but a tiny fraction of that vast host. Not one of those seven millions in all the countries of Europe and of the New World, but his death broke some tie of friendship, made a vacant place in some home, and the mourning for them will last with our lives. It is no use our asking that question which has so often come to the lips of disconsolate men and women, " Were their lives sacrificed in vain ? " " The true sorrow of humanity consists in this, not that the mind of man fails, but that the course and demands of actions and of life so rarely correspond with the dignity and intensity of human desires." So said Wordsworth more than a hundred years ago, and his words are as true now as when he wrote them.

To many the last five years have been a disenchant-ment. Every cloud has a silver lining, and we take

strength from the fact that, through all the difficulties of the time, the strength and moderation of
the character of our people has once again shown
itself, and in our country, almost alone in Europe,
have we had freedom from unconstitutional rebellion.
And more than that, I think we may say of our own
people that feelings of hatred and vengeance have
no permanent root in their hearts.

I think we ought to remember at a gathering like
this, that in the Civil Service, different perhaps from
many other services, only a limited number could
go and fight, and the Civil Service contained many
men who, had they been able, would have been in
the forefront of the battle, and who, not being able
to go, devoted themselves to the work of the country
in their various stations in a manner deserving of the
highest praise. Many lives were sacrificed in the
war, sacrificed under the strain of continuous overwork as truly and in the same spirit as those who
gave their lives in battle. Of no department can
that be said with greater truth than of this great
department to which we are proud to belong or to
have belonged.

Of those whose names we commemorate here,
" In the sight of the unwise, they seem to die :
and their departure is taken for misery, and their
going from us to be utter destruction : but they are
in peace." Peace is theirs, and we have to remember
that, and it is a peace that we cannot share. Lincoln
said, and I think his are words we should take from

here to-day, " We must show an increased devotion to that cause for which they gave the last full measure of devotion."

In many ways our task is the harder, for, after all the sorrows that most of us here have been through, we have to face the world with a high courage and brave heart for the allotted time that may be left, and devote ourselves each in his own vocation to the service of our common humanity, knowing well that it is only by the united efforts of men and women that we can maintain our civilisation at the level to which it has been raised, and that only by super-human effort can we better it. To try to do that is the least we can do for those who gave their lives for us. It is only in proportion as we go out into the world to do what we can for the world, that we can answer that question at the end and say, " They have not died in vain."

PRINTED IN GREAT BRITAIN BY ROBERT MACLEHOSE AND CO. LTD.
THE UNIVERSITY PRESS, GLASGOW.

PUBLISHER'S NOTE

OUR thanks are due to the Editors of
the *Times*, the *Morning Post*, the *Daily
Telegraph*, the *Yorkshire Post*, the
Student and the *English Race*, and to
Mr. John Murray for the permission
they have kindly given us to make
use of the texts of the Prime Minister's
addresses published by them.